T0326313

Research Tendencies and Prospect Domains for AI Development and Implementation

Published 2024 by River Publishers
River Publishers
Alsbjergvej 10, 9260 Gistrup, Denmark
www.riverpublishers.com

Distributed exclusively by Routledge
605 Third Avenue, New York, NY 10017, USA
4 Park Square, Milton Park, Abingdon, Oxon OX14 4RN

Research Tendencies and Prospect Domains for AI Development and Implementation /
by Yuriy P. Kondratenko, Anatolii I. Shevchenko.

Routledge is an imprint of the Taylor & Francis Group, an informa business

ISBN 978-87-7004-693-0 (paperback)

ISBN 978-87-7004-695-4 (online)

ISBN 978-8-770-04694-7 (ebook master)

A Publication in the River Publishers Series in Rapids

While every effort is made to provide dependable information, the publisher, authors, and editors cannot be held responsible for any errors or omissions.

Research Tendencies and Prospect Domains for AI Development and Implementation

Editors

Yuriy P. Kondratenko

Petro Mohyla Black Sea National University and
Institute of Artificial Intelligence Problems of Ministry of Education and
Science and National Academy of Sciences of Ukraine, Ukraine

Anatolii I. Shevchenko

Institute of Artificial Intelligence Problems of Ministry of Education and
Science and National Academy of Sciences of Ukraine, Ukraine

NEW YORK AND LONDON

Contents

3 Multivariate Information Systems and Polymetric Sensors: AI Implementation Perspective in Shipping and Shipbuilding   59

Yu. D. Zhukov and O. V. Zivenko

4 There is Still Plenty of Room at the Bottom: Feynman's Vision of Quantum Computing 65 Years Later   77

Alexis Lupo, Olga Kosheleva, Vladik Kreinovich,

Victor Timchenko, and Yuriy Kondratenko

5 Decision Support System for Maintenance Planning of Vortex Electrostatic Precipitators Based on IoT and AI Techniques   87

Lu Congxiang, Oleksiy Kozlov, Galyna Kondratenko,

and Anna Aleksieieva

Preface

This River Publishers Rapid book analyzes artificial intelligence (AI) implementation priorities, prospect domains as well as some new research tendencies and trends for AI development and implementation. The book consists of seven chapters in the AI field and may be conditionally divided into two parts.

Part 1 is devoted to the world's priorities in AI's implementation and its main components (Chapters 1 and 2) and is based on (a) analysis of the 50 national strategies for AI development as well as the world's and NATO's priorities in AI implementation; (b) methodological aspects for creating the Ukrainian AI conception and strategy, key priority areas for the introduction of AI in Ukraine, the conscience approach to AI systems design, as well as a discussion on new generation computer systems with embedded AI. Special attention is paid to perspectives of AI implementation in education and interrelation and inter-influence between AI and educational systems.

Part 2 (Chapters 3–7) is devoted to some new tendencies in AI development and implementation. Many scientific results and discussions are directed to some new trends in contemporary AI research: (a) AI systems and tools for shipping and shipbuilding; (b) quantum computing and color optical fuzzy computing in applied AI R&D; (c) AI for increasing the efficiency of the decision-making processes; (d) neural networks for solving classification and recognition tasks.

This book provides an overview of the recent developments in advanced AI systems including new theoretical findings and successful examples of practical implementation of the AI tools in different areas of human activities.

The monograph consists of research-analytic-oriented chapters presented by invited high-caliber scientists from different countries (Ukraine, the United States of America, Poland, Norway, and P.R. of China).

The chapter "Analysis of the Prospect Domains in AI Implementation: Nationals, NATO and Ukraine AI Strategies" presents an overview of the national AI strategies in different developed countries, NATO approaches and Ukrainian AI conception and strategy with focuses on the perspective domains of AI implementation. Special attention is paid to the analysis and example demonstrations of AI advances, challenges, and dangers as well as current steps in the AI regulation policy on the national and international levels.

The chapter "Interrelation and Inter-influence of Artificial Intelligence and Higher Education Systems" analyzes recent developments, applications, and perspectives of AI tools for increasing the efficiency of education processes. The important role of AI academia and academia/IT-industry consortia in training AI specialists, and sharing AI resources and qualified cadres is discussed in detail with examples of successful such type consortia in the USA, United Kingdom, Sweden, Thailand and Africa.

The chapter "Multivariate Information Systems and Polymetric Sensors: AI Implementation Perspective in Shipping and Shipbuilding" discusses the increasingly global impact of AI's methods and instruments on accelerating the dual transition of the maritime industry, including shipping, shipbuilding, and critical maritime infrastructure. The purpose of the research is a concise and structured review of some gaps in the development and implementation of the concepts of e-navigation, Digital Twins, Industrial Internet of Things, etc., and their potential influence on the safety and overall efficiency of commercial ships and onshore transshipment terminals.

The chapter "There is Still Plenty of Room at the Bottom: Feynman's Vision of Quantum Computing 65 Years Later" discusses the historical aspects of the appearing quantum computing and interrelation of quark computing and color optical computing as perspective tools (approaches) for creating advanced AI systems with further speed up computation processes.

The chapter "Decision Support System for Maintenance Planning of Vortex Electrostatic Precipitators Based on IoT and AI Techniques" addresses the issue of introducing an intelligent decision support system (DSS) for efficient maintenance planning of vortex electrostatic precipitators (VEPs) in industrial settings. Leveraging the integration of the Internet of Things and AI techniques, the proposed DSS aims to significantly reduce equipment downtime through the optimization of cleaning modes and schedules. In light of the increasing importance of production efficiency and continuous improvement of intelligent technologies, this study becomes particularly relevant as it offers a comprehensive solution for optimizing VEP performance using AI.

The chapter "Leveraging Pre-trained Neural Networks for Image Classification in Audio Signal Analysis for Mobile Applications of Home Automation" presents an in-depth analysis of innovative approaches in the field of audio signal classification using convolutional neural networks and their integration with image processing techniques. The authors investigate the effectiveness of transfer learning from image to audio domains, examining various neural network architectures like VGG16, DenseNet201, MobileNetV3Small, and EfficencyNet. Special emphasis is placed on the adaptability of these networks to handle audio data, particularly through the manipulation of input sizes and structures, such as Mel-frequency cepstral coefficients and short-time Fourier transform spectrograms.

The chapter "Effectiveness Evaluations of Optical Color Fuzzy Computing" describes the special AI technique for increasing the efficiency of fuzzy information processing. The proposed by the authors approach consists of representing input fuzzy information as color information quanta with the ability to carry out logical operations with them based on the transformation of light radiation. It is shown that the proposed approach provides obvious advantages of increasing the speed of logical calculations due to direct processing (without digitalization) of large fuzzy input data.

The chapters of the monograph have been structured to provide an easy-to-follow introduction to the topics that are addressed, including the most relevant references, so that anyone interested in this field can get started in the area.

This book may be useful for researchers, policymakers, and students who are interested in creating strategies for AI research, development and implementation, and developing advanced AI tools and systems.

Let us express our deep appreciation to all authors for their contributions as well as to reviewers for their timely and interesting comments and suggestions. We certainly look forward to working with all contributors again shortly.

14 February, 2024

Yuriy P. Kondratenko

Anatolii I. Shevchenko

About the Editors

 **Yuriy Kondratenko** is a Doctor of Science, Professor, Honour Inventor of Ukraine (2008), Corr. Academician of the Royal Academy of Doctors (Barcelona, Spain), Corr. Academician of the Royal Academy of Economic and Finance Sciences (Spain), Head of the Department of Intelligent Information Systems at Petro Mohyla Black Sea National University (PMBSNU), Ukraine, Leading Researcher of the Institute of Artificial Intelligence Problems of MES and NAS of Ukraine, Fulbright Scholar. He has received a Ph.D. (1983) and Dr.Sc. (1994) at Odessa National Polytechnic University, and several international grants and scholarships for conducting research at P.R. of China, Germany, and the USA. He is Guest Editor of 3 Special Issue of River Publishers Journal of Mobile Multimedia and an Editor of several River Publishers monographs, including Advances in Intelligent Robotics and Collaborative Automation (2015), Control Systems: Theory and Applications (2018), Advanced Control Systems: Theory and Applications (2021), and Recent Developments in Automatic Control Systems (2022). Research interests include artificial intelligence, robotics, automation, sensors and control systems, intelligent decision support systems, and fuzzy logic.

 **Anatolii Shevchenko** graduated from the Faculty of Physics at Donetsk State University with a major in Radio Physics and Electronics. In 1985, he defended his Ph.D. thesis and in 1990 he received the academic degree of Doctor of Technical Sciences. In 1997, he was awarded the title of professor, and in 1998 the honorary title of Honored Scientist and Technician of Ukraine. In 2006, was elected as a Corresponding Member of the National Academy of Sciences of Ukraine in the field of Computer Systems. In 2015, he was appointed as the Director of the Institute of Artificial Intelligence of the Ministry of Education and Science of Ukraine and the National Academy of Sciences of Ukraine in Kyiv. Together with the Department of Informatics of the National Academy of Sciences of Ukraine, he initiated an international scientific journal called "Artificial Intelligence" and was appointed as its chief editor. His research interests encompass various aspects of artificial intelligence, modeling human intelligence, simulating elements of human consciousness, breakthrough technologies in the field of artificial intelligence, and multidisciplinary aspects of artificial intelligence.

CHAPTER

1

Analysis of the Prospect Domains in AI Implementation: Nationals, NATO and Ukraine AI Strategies

A. I. Shevchenko[1], Y. P. Kondratenko[1,2], V. I. Slyusar[1,], I. P. Atamanyuk[3], G. V. Kondratenko[2*], and T. V. Yeroshenko[1]

[1]Institute of Artificial Intelligence Problems of MES and NAS of Ukraine, Kyiv, Ukraine
[2]Intelligent Information Systems Department, Petro Mohyla Black Sea National University, Mykolaiv, Ukraine
[3]Warsaw University of Life Sciences, Warsaw, Poland
E-mail: rektor_iai@ukr.net, y_kondrat2002@yahoo.com, swadim@ukr.net, ihor_atamaniuk@sggw.edu.pl, halyna.kondratenko@chmnu.edu.ua, eroshenko@ipai.net.ua
*Corresponding Author

Abstract

This chapter is devoted to the implementation aspects of artificial intelligence (AI) based on the analysis of 50 national strategies for AI development in developed countries. The different forms of national AI presentations and prospect domains for AI applications are discussed. Special attention is paid to NATO and Ukraine activities in AI development and implementation at the current stage and in the future. The chapter focuses on the modern advantages in AI development and challenges in AI implementation including moral-ethical issues and dangers for human civilization. Some character examples of AI implementation in positive and negative aspects are considered as the basis for creating national and world policies in the regulation of AI development and implementation.

Keywords: Artificial intelligence, strategies, development, implementation, advances, challenges, regulation policy.

1.1 Introduction

Artificial intelligence (AI) plays a decisive role in the modern stage of innovative development of technologically developed countries of the world. Methods and means of artificial intelligence are widely used in various areas of human activity [1, 2], such as medicine, manufacturing, agriculture, the country's defense, state administration, the space industry, and others.

Successful examples of the use of artificial intelligence in various countries of the world [3] confirm the possibility of a significant increase in economic indicators due to the creation of opportunities for a more effective solution for complex technical, economic, social, and humanitarian tasks.

AI has enormous potential and is the engine of global progressive development. This technology can help tackle challenges such as combating climate change, fighting against terrorism, discovering and developing new methods of diagnosis and treatment of oncological and cardiovascular diseases, optimization of automated industrial processes, increasing efficiency in education, and others.

Many publications are devoted to AI development and implementation in different fields, to describing successful cases, AI advances and AI influence on crucial decisions and shaping new perspectives on the future [4–7]. Today's key goal is to ensure efficient and transparent research in human-centered AI systems and an effective governance framework for AI implementation processes.

The efforts of researchers, governors, and policymakers must be directed to the adaptation of AI's potential to improve the lives of people and create a corresponding atmosphere and innovative conditions for AI development and implementation for a happy future of the people. The scientific community needs to constantly analyze and understand not only advances but also the challenges and dangers of wide AI implementation as well as develop and standardize approaches for AI research to take into account potential threats arising from unethical or uncontrolled behaviors of designers and users [3, 8].

The aim and focus of this chapter is the analysis of (a) the strategic plans in developing perspective AI technologies, (b) the main priority domains in AI implementation in the different regions of the world, and (c) the potential dangers and important ethical issues concerning AI development and implementation.

The remainder of the chapter is presented in the following way. Section 1.2 discusses the different forms and peculiarities of the national AI strategies for the main developed countries in the world. The NATO perspectives and directions in AI development and implementation are considered in Section 1.3. The conception, main prospect domains and plans for creating and implementing AI in Ukraine is discussed in Section 1.4. Section 1.5 is devoted to the analysis of the advantages, challenges, and dangers of AI implementation for people, countries, ecology, and others. The current state of creating regulatory policy in the AI field is considered in Section 1.6. Finally, Section 1.7 concludes the study and suggests potential directions for forthcoming research.

1.2 Priorities in AI Implementation Based on National Strategies

Investment in AI development and implementation is growing year by year in all regions of the world. According to experts, the implementation of AI is predicted by 2030 to increase the gross domestic product (GDP) of China, in particular, by 26%, in North America by 14%, and in Europe by around 10% [2, 3].

The rank of AI implementation in the different domains of human activity will play a significant role in the scientific-economical competition between countries, companies, and regions on the global world level and their leadership. Understanding this concept, the governments of different countries try to underline the importance of AI development and implementation by creating national AI strategies with a focus on the priorities in research, creation, and application of AI systems, taking into account their national peculiarities, national interests, and current state of science, education and the countries' economy as a whole.

A list of 50 developed countries, which represent 90% of the global GDP, was published by Holon IQ and included countries that officially presented their national strategies for AI development and implementation [9, 10]. Practically, the countries from all continents are presented in this list. It is very important to underline that national AI strategies in different countries have different forms, all national strategies were created without general unification and standardization approaches and correspondingly all 50 national AI strategies can be divided into several groups depending on the forms of AI strategy presentation. Some of them are in the form of an AI roadmap, plan, program, initiative, white paper, executive order, etc. Table 1.1 presents information about the form of the national AI strategies in different countries and groups of countries.

Table 1.1: The form of national AI strategies in different groups of countries.

Form of the national AI strategy	Country
AI roadmap	Australia, the Netherlands, the Philippines
AI national programme	Finland, Singapore, Saudi Arabia
AI plan	Argentina, China, Poland, United States of America
AI strategy	Belgium, Brazil, Canada, Czech Republic, Denmark, Estonia, France, Germany, Hungary, India, Indonesia, Japan, Kenya, Lithuania, Luxemburg, Malta, Mexico, Norway, Qatar, South Korea, Spain, Tunisia and others
AI white paper	Italy
AI mission	Austria
National AI initiative	Portugal, South Africa
AI national approach	Spain
AI policy	Chile, Colombia
Presidential AI initiative	Pakistan
AI report	New Zealand, United Kingdom
AI framework	Malaysia
Recommendation for AI strategy	Sweden
Executive order on AI	Russia

Canada and Japan were the first and second countries in the world, respectively, that created and introduced their national strategies for AI development and implementation [3, 9, 10]. Each national AI strategy reflects the main domains and priorities in AI development and implementation, taking into account the unique economic and geographical characteristics of each country, the interconnection between industrial and agricultural sectors, the correlation between science and education, and expected and desired transformations in corresponding areas of human activity.

Let us analyze the priority domains and priority goals for AI development and implementation based on the national AI strategies of several countries from different continents (Asia, Africa, North America, South America, Europe, and Australia).

Among the priority domains of AI implementation [3, 9, 10] are: health, infrastructure and natural resources (Australia); research and innovation, society, ethics and labor market, qualification and training, AI governance, security and law, AI in the public sector, infrastructure for industrial leadership positions, AI in the economy (Austria); research and talent development (Canada); human capital, fiber optic networks, computing infrastructure, ethics, standards, security, and regulation (Chile); R&D, industrialization, talent development, education and skills acquisition, standard setting and regulations, ethical norms, and security (China); financial inclusion, cybersecurity, land tilting, the election process, single digital identity, and overall public service delivery (Kenya); AI in the public delivery (Kenya); AI in the public sector and business based on regulation and data access, infrastructure and information-communication technologies; realization of the ethical principles, protection of data and security (Norway); education based on special training programs and AI graduate schools, health, public safety, and defense based on funding major projects, infrastructure based on AI semiconductors for autonomous vehicles (South Korea); the education domain for training more skilled AI professionals; the science domain for creating significant results in applied and fundamental AI research based on ethical, safe, reliable, and transparent AI developments (Sweden); transport, health, space, renewable energy, water, technology, education, environment and traffic (United Arab Emirates).

Among the main goals for AI development and implementation are [1, 2, 9, 10]: (a) policy support on ethics, regulation, skills, and competencies; provide AI cartography; co-animate Belgian AI community; collect EU funding and connect EU ecosystems; training in AI; implementation AI technologies to the industries; new products and services based on AI technologies (Belgium); (b) concentrate research on developing responsible and trusted AI, promote digital transformation for SME (small and medium-sized enterprises), enhance economic development, ensure equitable distribution of AI benefits (Czech Republic); (c) to make digital transformation of business and providing the necessary digital skills to people (Denmark); (d) advancing the AI implementation in the public and private sector, developing AI R&D, education and a legal environment for the AI introduction (Estonia); (e) enhance the skills for searching the quality jobs, invest in research and domains that can provide the maximization of economic growth and social impact, and wide introduction of Indian-made AI developments to other developing countries (India); (f) increasing number of young researchers in AI fields and unifying data formats and standards for different industrial sectors (Japan); (g) crime prediction in the public sector, improving services for citizens and internal government processes (Lithuania); (h) building up AI talent, integrating ethics in AI frameworks, R&D investment, and balancing the role of man and machine (the Netherlands); (i) creating job places and an AI ecosystem for equitable and sustainable development (Tunisia); investing in AI research, unleashing AI resources, setting AI governance standards, building the AI workforce, and protecting the American AI advantages (United States of America).

As we can see, many priority goals and priority domains (transport, education, health, and others) are common for the national AI strategies of the corresponding groups of countries and, at the same time, many countries demonstrate specific and unique goals and priority domains for AI development and implementation.

Experts estimated [11] that by 2030 the contribution of AI to the global economy will be $15.7 trillion (US dollars).

1.3 NATO's Priorities and Perspectives in AI Implementation

It is necessary to underline that AI's solutions have become a significant integral part of national security strengthening and an important component of warfare operations [2], especially at the last stage of quick development of various intelligent technologies and multidisciplinary research.

AI can offer a wide spectrum of military applications for providing strategic and tactical advantages. In particular, the war in Ukraine has become the first high-tech war in human history, in which both sides of the conflict began utilizing the capabilities of computational artificial intelligence. Ukrainian forces, during the Russian invasion of Ukraine, implemented modern AI technologies for battlefield intelligence, counterpropaganda, and communication interception across various channels [12] and others.

The UK pays a lot of attention to using AI for the modernization of its defense weapons [3]. The integration of AI is the basis for the implementation of an upgrading strategy for the UK defense program, which was unveiled in June 2022. According to this strategy, a centralized defense AI center for research, development, and implementation was established and a part of military capital funds is planned for direct financial support of civilian AI projects with dual assignment.

Germany, for deployment and activation of scientific research and technological investigations based on the AI development and implementation, has dedicated euros 500 million (June 2022).

The US Department of Defense has asked (for the research and development of advanced AI-connected technologies) for a sum of US $874 million as part of the 2022 US military budget.

Such examples of the organizational and financial activity and support of USA, Germany and UK demonstrate that NATO member states have recognized the significant potential of AI to transform their defense strategies, streamline operations, and enhance military capabilities [1, 2]. Striving to maintain a competitive advantage on the world stage, NATO countries prioritize AI research and implementation to increase interoperability and ensure a safer and more sustainable future. NATO, in July 2022, announced a euros 1 billion venture investment dedicated to technology investments, including AI [3].

Some publications consider the key priorities of AI research and implementation in NATO countries [1, 2, 3, 13, 14], and analyze the challenges and opportunities presented by this modern disruptive technology. Topics such as strategic planning, force optimization, information advantage, and ethical aspects are also discussed, highlighting how NATO members can effectively use AI to strengthen their defenses and contribute to international security. When considering the current landscape of AI in the military domain, an important focus is also on cooperation and interaction between NATO allies to achieve common goals and protect against potential threats.

To coordinate efforts in the field of AI technologies, the NATO Data and AI Review Board (DARB) was created. DARB began its work on AI standardization in February 2023 with the implementation of an initiative to develop a comprehensive and accessible certification standard for artificial intelligence. This standard aims to ensure that the industries and institutions of the Alliance meet international legal standards, as well as the principles and values of NATO [15].

The NATO Science and Technology Organization published "Science & Technology Trends 2023–2043" across the Physical, Biological, and Information Domains with the priorities of AI development and implementation for the years 2023–2043 [16].

Among the disruptive technologies, the authors of the overview in [16] consider big data, information and communication technologies, artificial intelligence, robotics and autonomous systems, space, hypersonics, energy and propulsions, electronics, and electromagnetics. Quantum, bio, and human enhancement technologies are included in the group of emergent technologies.

At the same time, the most disruptive and emergent technologies are interconnected between each other based on convergence, inter-dependencies and synergies, and special attention in [16] is paid to data-AI-autonomy, data-quantum, space-hypersonics-materials, space-quantum, data-AI-biotechnologies, data-AI-materials, and energy-materials AI. As another example, NATO's Quantum Technologies Strategy talks about the need to take into account the consequences of the development of data and artificial intelligence for quantum technologies [17]. It is also necessary to underline that special research should be directed at solving complex problems associated with human–AI teaming and psycho-socio-technical issues.

NATO specialists use the AI definition, which was published by the Air Force Research Laboratory (AFRL) in [18], in particular:

"AI refers to the ability of machines to perform tasks that normally require human intelligence – for example, recognizing patterns, learning from experience, drawing conclusions, making predictions, or taking action – whether digitally or as the smart software behind autonomous physical systems".

AI is seen by NATO analysts as a technology to improve operational awareness by processing and integrating data from various sensors, platforms, and intelligence sources in real time. AI tools can help a more complete understanding and prediction of potential risks, adversary intentions, and the impact of various strategic decisions as well as detecting anomalies or suspicious activity, informing decision-makers on potential dangers, and laying the groundwork for a faster and more targeted response.

AI can also be used to model the behavior of adversaries, giving NATO countries a better understanding of their actions and reactions in various scenarios.

The authors in [16] discuss some of the more exciting and potentially disruptive AI applications concerning artificial social intelligence, automating disinformation and cognitive warfare strategies, producing and identifying "deep fakes," supplementing air or air-weapons control, aiding in high-resolution image recognition, creating images from text descriptions, navigating human terrain, and providing universal (low usage) language translation.

On the other hand, AI technologies are an organic ecosystem for analyzing current NATO capabilities inside the NATO Defense Planning Process (NDPP) [1, 2, 13] and more effective identification of shortcomings.

NDPP [1, 2, 13] may be considered a key mechanism that manages the development of NATO's military capabilities, ensuring the Alliance's readiness and ability to respond to new security challenges. In this regard, processing and evaluating data from various sources with the help of AI can provide a comprehensive overview of the Alliance's strengths and weaknesses, indicating areas that require improvement or investment. This can help NATO countries make informed decisions about the development and prioritization of force capabilities.

In addition, the identified gaps are the basis for specifying or forming new requirements for the minimum capabilities of forces (minimal capability requirements).

An effective tool that can help analysts in this process is the large language models (LLM) of AI. As an example, their ability to generate relevant proposals is illustrated in Figures 1.1 and 1.2, where the response of GPT-4 regarding the lethality of the soldier is given and the distribution of the corresponding fire lines according to the representation of GPT-4 is illustrated.

As everyone can see, the conclusions provided by GPT-4 are quite relevant and can inspire the relevant thoughts of experts regarding the formalization of requirements for the lethal capabilities of a unit or a platoon of soldiers.

This is quite important because now, the lack of analytical resources does not allow to advance the NDPP process to the company and platoon level of soldiers, limiting it to the battalion level.

Effective allocation of resources and optimization of military forces are vital for NATO countries to maintain their strategic advantage. AI-based systems can help streamline these processes, ensuring the efficient and effective use of assets across various areas and branches of military command.

In particular, the use of AI can reduce the cognitive burden of commanders with the help of personal LLM assistants [19]. On the tactical level, an application of large language models such as GPT-4 can significantly enhance the efficiency of various tasks performed by soldiers. For instance, LLMs can automate reporting and documentation, generating situational reports and filling out standard forms and documents, which greatly reduces time spent on bureaucratic processes. They support decision-making by analyzing large volumes of data, including combat reports, to provide recommendations and

Figure 1.1: A fragment of the GPT-4 proposals (answer) for the lethality of a soldier: SW – expert question.

 What are requirements to the letality distance of fire of small arms in squad level?

 The lethality distance requirements for small arms at the squad level may vary depending on the military organization, mission objectives, and specific operational environment. However, some general guidelines can be applied to ensure that squads have effective engagement capabilities across various distances:

1. Close Range (0-100 meters): Soldiers must be proficient in engaging targets at close range using personal weapons, such as assault rifles or submachine guns. These weapons are typically chambered in intermediate calibers (e.g., 5.56x45mm NATO, 7.62x39mm) and offer a good balance of controllability, accuracy, and stopping power for close-range engagements.

2. Medium Range (100-300 meters): Effective engagement at medium range often relies on the use of assault rifles or designated marksman rifles (DMRs). These weapons provide greater accuracy and range than close-range personal weapons and are often equipped with optics to facilitate better target acquisition and engagement.

Figure 1.2: A generalized result of the recommended GPT-4 distribution distances of fire damage from small arms.

	Close Range	Medium Range	Long Range	Suppressive Fire	Anti-material Anti-Vehicle Fire
		7.62x39 5.56x45	7.62x51 0.338		0.5 BMG 12.7x108 14.5x114
	< 100 m	100–300 m	300–800 m	< 1000 m	< 1500 m

support commanders in decision-making. LLMs are also useful in creating training materials and instructions and conducting virtual training sessions.

In terms of medical support, they can provide first-aid instructions, interpret symptoms, and offer treatment recommendations. Their ability to translate languages and texts facilitates communication with local populations or international partners without a language barrier. LLMs are also instrumental in planning and logistics, analyzing and optimizing logistical routes, task planning, and resource allocation. They can be used for image recognition and intelligent data analysis, identifying important objects such as enemy equipment or changes in the landscape.

LLMs offer psychological support, including stress management and counseling. They are capable of performing accurate ballistic calculations and providing up-to-date weather information. Additionally, LLMs can be used to create augmented reality (AR) applications for visualization and mission planning.

As information superiority and strong cyber defense capabilities are critical in an increasingly interconnected world, a priority for AI development is to help NATO countries achieve these goals by strengthening their intelligence, surveillance, and reconnaissance capabilities, as well as strengthening their cyber defenses. AI-based systems can analyze massive amounts of data to detect cyber threats and intrusions, respond in real time, and even predict and prevent future attacks. Additionally, AI can support information operations, such as disinformation campaigns and psychological operations, to counter an adversary's narratives and impact on target audiences.

With the increasing dependence of NATO countries on AI for military purposes, they must inevitably face the ethical aspects and ensure the responsible use of AI. The development and deployment of AI-based weapons systems raises questions about accountability, transparency, and potential unintended consequences. NATO countries cooperate to establish common ethical standards and principles governing the use of AI in defense and invest in scientific research to minimize bias, improve explanatory power, and ensure the technology's compliance with international humanitarian law and principles of human rights.

Finally, AI offers NATO countries enormous potential for revolutionary changes in military strategies and capabilities. By prioritizing strategic planning, force optimization, information dominance, and ethical aspects, NATO will be able to realize the full potential of AI and strengthen collective security. Collaboration and cooperation among NATO allies to confront complex challenges and threats will be crucial along the way.

Among 10 countries in the world (100%) with the highest level of AI development and implementation according to STEAM analysis for 2018–2021 are 6 countries that are NATO members [16], in particular, United States of America (41%), United Kingdom (11%), Germany (10%), France (5%), Canada (5%) and Italy (4%).

Among the 10 leading institutions in the world [16] in the AI field according to a STEAM analysis for 2018–2021 are 7 institutions from the NATO-member countries [16], in particular, Max Planck Society, Harvard University, University of Cambridge, Stanford University, University of Oxford, Massachusetts Institute of Technology and University of Michigan.

NATO has perspective relations with Ukraine and constantly supports Ukraine in this wartime during the Russian invasion of this independent country. In May 2023, the Minister of Digital Transformation of Ukraine, Mykhailo Fedorov, during a meeting in Brussels with Deputy Secretary General of the Alliance David van Wiel, announced [20] that NATO scientists will help Ukrainian developers in the field of military innovations.

1.4 Conception and Strategy of AI Development in Ukraine

Ukraine holds an active position in the global market for AI technologies. Ukraine is among the top three countries in Eastern Europe for the number of operating AI companies.

The conception for AI development and implementation in Ukraine [21] was created based on the initiative of the Ministry of Digital Transformation of Ukraine and approved by the Cabinet of Ministers of Ukraine in December 2020. This conception describes the main purpose, principles, and tasks of the development of artificial intelligence technologies in Ukraine as one of the priority directions in the field of scientific and technological research.

Implementation of the conception is foreseen for the period until 2030. The priority domains for AI implementation according to the conception for AI development and implementation in Ukraine are: (a) increasing contribution of Ukraine and occupying a significant segment of the world market of AI technologies and leading positions in international rankings; (b) active participitation in the implementation of international initiatives on AI development, regulation and standardization; (c) implementation of AI technologies in the field of education, economy, public administration, cyber security, defense and other areas to ensure the long-term competitiveness of Ukraine on the international market; (d) providing access to information (databases, electronic registers, etc.), its use during the development of AI technologies for the production of goods and the provision of services; (e) promoting the dissemination of research results in the field of AI and improving their quality; (f) increasing the level of professional training of specialists to ensure the field of AI technologies has qualified personnel; (g) protection of the information space from unauthorized intervention, ensuring the safe functioning of information and telecommunication systems; (h) increasing the level of public safety through the use of AI technologies during the development of resocialization measures for convicted persons and the risk of reoffending; (i) bringing the legislation in the field of using AI technologies into compliance with international legal acts.

The main priority areas for Ukraine in which the tasks of the state policy for AI development and implementation are [21]: education and professional training, science, economy, cyber security, information security, defense, public administration, legal regulation and ethics, and justice.

The Institute of Problems of Artificial Intelligence of the National Academy of Sciences and the Ministry of Education and Science of Ukraine [22] became the initiator and main organization for the implementation of the project on the creation of the Strategy for the Development of Artificial Intelligence in Ukraine, which was carried out in 2020 and 2021 with the involvement of leading specialists and scientists in the field of artificial intelligence from all over Ukraine.

During the work on the project, various proposals of the project participants were born and optimized, the introduced concepts and definitions were polished, critical remarks and comments were made regarding the structure of the document and the content of individual sections, the conclusions of the experienced experts involved in the examination of the project, who were not the authors of the project, were processed.

The main sections of the final version of the project Strategy for the Development of Artificial Intelligence in Ukraine are the following:

(1) Paradigm of artificial intelligence.
(2) Basic concepts and directions of research in the field of artificial intelligence.
(3) The purpose and objectives of the National Strategy for the Development of Artificial Intelligence in Ukraine.
(4) The state of development of artificial intelligence in Ukraine.
(5) World's standards of artificial intelligence.
(6) System of management and regulation of artificial intelligence in Ukraine.

(7)   Scientific, personnel, and material support of the national ecosystem of artificial intelligence.

(8)   Artificial intelligence in priority areas of development of Ukraine.

(9)   Assessment of changes in the labor market in Ukraine under the influence of the development of artificial intelligence.

(10)   Final provisions of the Strategy for the Development of Artificial Intelligence in Ukraine in 2026–2030.

Public discussion around the project "Strategy for Artificial Intelligence Development in Ukraine" [22, 23] commenced towards the end of 2021.

Besides the abovementioned priority domains described in the AI conception, the project of the AI strategy includes such priority areas as medicine, agriculture, industry and energy, transport and infrastructure, ecology, and environmental protection.

At the current time, Ukraine actively implements advanced AI technologies in the different domains, for example: (a) for creating AI-based autonomous drones and robots [24, 25, 26, 27, 28, 29, 30]: (1) Highland Systems, a company founded by Ukrainians, presented a prototype of the radar-invisible electric unmanned submarine Kronos [25], the drone can move silently at speeds of up to 50 km/h and launch torpedoes; (2) more than 200 Ukrainian companies are involved in the production of UAVs [26]; (3) on 24 October 2023, the ground kamikaze robot Ratel S, created by Ukrainian developers Brave1, successfully passed field tests and was put into mass production [27]. The Ukrainian Defense Forces will use the Ratel S as a mobile warhead carrying anti-tank mines or a combat module. An operator from a safe location can blow up an enemy tank or dugout. The maximum speed of the drone reaches 24 kilometers, and the range of use is 6 kilometers. Ratel S can work up to 2 hours without recharging; (b) Railway Company "Ukrzaliznytsia" [31] has begun to use ChatGPT to analyze passenger appeals. During the day, the app receives an average of 1300 travel ratings from passengers. About 300 of them are text reviews about the railway. Artificial intelligence will distribute passenger appeals on 21 topics, from service quality to delays. Currently, ChatGPT correctly determines the category of the request in 90% of cases; (c) The Ministry of Digitization is developing a virtual assistant in "Diya" [32], the task of which is to quickly find answers to users' questions. In addition, AI will help the State Statistics Service to process and analyze data; (d) Some benefits of AI implementation are in military technologies [32] as AI helps to record the movement of enemy equipment and personnel, to shoot down missiles, to target UAVs more effectively, etc.; (e) Ukraine uses AI technologies (face recognition) to search for missing citizens during the full-scale Russian war [33]; (f) the National Agency for the Prevention of Corruption has decided that artificial intelligence will help verify the declarations of officials [34]. All submitted declarations will undergo a risk assessment. Those declarations that will have the lowest risk rating indicator and can be checked automatically will be able to be checked by artificial intelligence – an automated check mechanism.

The "Strategy for Artificial Intelligence Development in Ukraine" pays special attention to such a "breakthrough" direction of AI research as designing AI systems based on the concept of consciousness and conscience (Figure 1.3) [1, 2, 3, 35, 36, 37].

Figure 1.3: Components of the new generation computer system based on embedded AI

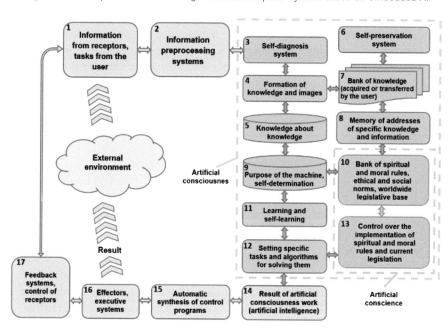

Figure 1.3 presents the main components of the integrated AI system, which is the basis for further research on AI in a personal context [38], for getting and preliminary processing sensor information, formation of patterns, and interaction with different memory units for real-time control of system functioning based on existing laws, rules and moral-ethical norms of the human-centered society [1, 2, 3, 24, 35, 38].

1.5 Advantages, Challenges and Potential Dangerousness of AI Development

Implementation of AI has many advantages for growing the economy and increasing research, industry, health and education potentials but, at the same time, some challenges, disadvantages, and dangers of AI implementation for humans, ecology, health, and others need to be dealt with.

Let us consider some examples of successful AI implementation in different fields of human activity.

Case 1. The Event Horizon Telescope (EHT) network captured a picture of the black hole at the center of the galaxy Messier 87, located more than 53 million light-years from Earth. It was in 2017, but the researchers managed to improve the image thanks to the use of AI in 2023 [39]. To improve the image, a new PRIMO method was used. PRIMO is an AI that learns to restore high-quality images even from fuzzy or without enough input data. Generative adversarial networks [40, 41, 42] were used for the generation of additional images for training. Trained on generated simulations of more than 30,000 black holes, the AI used data based on the knowledge of the physical laws of the universe, including black holes, to create more accurate pictures from the raw data obtained in 2017.

Case 2. An AI fighter pilot beat an experienced human pilot 15:0 in the Defense Advanced Research Projects Agency's AlphaDogfight competition [43]. The AI pilot didn't just fly better than the human did, it fought differently. Heron Systems' AI agent used forward-quarter gunshots when the two aircraft were racing toward each other head-to-head, a shot that's banned in pilot training because of the risk of a collision. AI in this case demonstrates a "superhuman capability" to make high-precision, split-second shots that were "almost impossible" for humans. Even more impressive, the AI system was not programmed to fight this way. It learned this tactic all on its own. AI systems' ability to perform not just better than humans, but to fight differently, is a major potential advantage in warfare.

Case 3. Organizers of the French Open tennis championship suggested that players at the tournament connect with AI Bodyguard [44] to filter offensive comments on social networks. AI Bodyguard can moderate comments in real-time, replies are analyzed in less than 200 milliseconds, and offensive comments are blocked.

Case 4. Japanese electronics company NEC is developing a wrist-based device to improve driving safety that can recognize the driver's emotions, including detecting the driver's excitement, nervousness, and severe fatigue

[45]. The information obtained will help transport and logistics companies improve traffic safety. NEC plans to put this AI technology into practice in 2025.

Case 5. The Albanian government wants to use ChatGPT [46] to translate thousands of pages of EU integration legislation into Albanian and then integrate them into the country's current legislation. It is about the coordination of 280 thousand pages of documents. With the help of ChatGPT, Albania can save on "an army of translators and a battalion of lawyers", whose services would cost millions of euros. The AI will translate into Albanian and provide a detailed overview of where and what changes need to be made to local legislation to align it with EU legislation. It must also analyze the impact of all measures and changes, which usually require many experts and a lot of time.

Case 6. British AI firm Luminance developed an AI system "Autopilot" [47] based on its proprietary LLM to automatically analyze and make changes to contracts. It was the first case in the world when AI demonstrated the ability to negotiate a contract autonomously with another AI without any human involvement in a matter of minutes.

Case 7. California firefighters use AI as part of the ALERTCalifornia AI program to detect wildfires by streaming real-time video from more than 1000 cameras located throughout the state [48]. In particular, the AI system noticed a fire that broke out at 3 a.m. local time in a remote, overgrown with bushes area in the Cleveland National Forest. AI reported to the fire service and the fire was extinguished after 45 minutes. ALERTCalifornia AI was developed by engineers at the University of California in San Diego using artificial intelligence from the DigitalPath Company. In addition to the network of cameras, the platform collects a huge amount of additional information, including aerial photography to quantify vegetation where future fires may occur and mapping of the Earth's surface.

It is possible to discuss many successful AI applications but we need also to pay attention to the challenges, disadvantages, and dangers of AI implementation at the current stage and in the future.

Let us consider several examples and case studies:

- According to a report by the British National Cyber Security Center, AI technology threatens the British parliamentary elections [49], which should be held in late 2024 to early 2025. This is because AI facilitates the spread of disinformation, in particular through fake videos and "hyperrealistic bots".
- Photographer Borys Eldagsen submitted a work created by artificial intelligence to the prestigious international Sony World Photography

Award photo contest and won in the "Creative" category [50]. He also immediately refused the award, admitting that his competition photo was created by artificial intelligence.

- Journalists have discovered that pedophiles are using AI to create and sell realistic material of child sexual abuse, including infant rape [51]. The creators of these images use Stable Diffusion as AI software, which was targeted to generate images for further use in art and graphic design. AI technology allows users to describe any desired image and then generate it.

- In South Korea, in the center of the distribution of agricultural products in the city of Goseong [52], an industrial robot, due to a configuration error, mistook a 40-year-old worker for a box of vegetables and killed this worker, who was checking the industrial robot's sensors.

- ChatGPT falsely accused George Washington University law professor Jonathan Turley of sexual harassment, adding him to a list of teachers involved in sex scandals [53]. The AI chat room (with citation of a non-existent article from The Washington Post) alleged that Turley made sexually suggestive comments and attempted to touch a female student during a field trip to Alaska. But Professor Turley never went to Alaska and was not accused of harassment or assault. He told "USA" Today about this and also drew attention to the dangers of defamation and misinformation from artificial intelligence.

The analysis of the advantages, disadvantages, challenges, and dangers of AI reveals its substantial impact on the economies of various countries, particularly on the labor market. Indeed, the world labor market will be seriously changed according to rapid AI development. The automation of part of working processes (expert forecast 10–40% in Europe) [3] can require significant transformations in rows of different professions. According to the report of the World Economic Forum (WEF), over the next five years [54] nearly a quarter of all jobs will be transformed by AI, digitalization, and other economic developments. Simultaneously, AI will lead to significant positive changes in the labor market. In particular, the impact of most AI-based technologies will be positive over the next five years, with big data analytics, management technology, and cybersecurity emerging as the biggest drivers of employment growth. In addition, the emergence of AI applications such as LLMs (ChatGPT, Minerva, and others) will allow the displacement and automation of many roles that involve reasoning, communication, and coordination. For instance, one of the largest newspapers in Germany, the tabloid Bild, will replace humans with artificial intelligence in several editorial positions [55]. Artificial intelligence will replace live workers as part of a 100 million euro cost-cutting program. Hundreds of layoffs are expected. This will concern the employees whose tasks are performed by artificial intelligence and/or automated processes in the digital world.

AI will have a lasting impact on practically every industry [3] and is expected to affect around 60% of businesses. Now, it is possible to see AI implementation in smart devices, cars, healthcare systems, and favorite apps and AI influence permeates deeper into many other industries. AI's influence on sectors is increasing and its impact on achieving sustainable development goals is crucial. Proper regulation and oversight are necessary to ensure transparency, safety, and ethical standards for sustainable development. AI's transformative potential on work varies by country, with distinct consequences across regions and industries.

The International Labor Organization (ILO) [56] believes that generative artificial intelligence is more likely to expand the work responsibilities of people by automating some processes than to destroy jobs and take over all work. The organization suggests that most jobs and industries are only partially amenable to automation and will most likely be supplemented rather than replaced by the latest wave of generative AI tools. According to the ILO, the biggest impact of AI technologies will probably not be the destruction of jobs, but rather the potential changes in the quality of work, including work intensity and autonomy. It follows from the organization's research that new technologies have the greatest impact on the field of office management (office work). In high-income countries, automation could potentially affect 5.5% of all emplo-yed people. In low-income countries, the risk of automation is only about 0.4%.

It is crucial to emphasize the potential risks associated with the development and deployment of AI weapons [57], in particular uncontrolled AI weapons that make decisions about killing on their own. Russia's war in Ukraine, using semi-autonomous drones and rockets, demonstrates how the future creation of AI lethal autonomous weapons (based on quadcopters, tanks, speedboats, submarines, humanoid robots, etc.) may be dangerous for humankind [57] and why scientists and progressive people must fight for the prohibition of AI weapons.

1.6 Regulation Policy in the AI Field

Taking into account the serious challenges and potential dangers of AI implementation and application of AI tools for negative goals a lot of outstanding scientists, CEOs of companies, and governments of countries are worried about that and have proposed some realistic steps for creating regulation policies in AI development and implementation on the national and international levels.

In particular, Geoffrey Hinton, who has been called the "godfather" of AI, left Google and underlined the risks of AI and the dangers of the development [58] he paved the way for. Hinton regrets his life's work and officially joined the ranks of critics who expressed concern about AI concerning both the speed at which it is developing and the direction in which it is moving. He also mentioned "bad actors" who would try to use AI for "bad things". The scientist warned that eventually, AI could create sub-goals like "I need to get more power".

The members of the Future of Life Institute wrote an open letter demanding the suspension of experiments with AI because AI systems that compete with human intelligence can pose serious risks to society and humanity [59]. Among them are the CEO of SpaceX, Tesla and X (Twitter) Elon Musk, Apple co-founder Steve Wozniak, Pinterest co-founder Evan Sharp, Skype co-founder Jaan Tallinn and more than 1000 other people who understand that advanced AI can cause profound changes in the history of life on Earth and should be planned and managed with due care and allocation of appropriate resources. The open letter calls on all AI labs to immediately pause for at least 6 months the training of AI systems more powerful than GPT-4.

AI is poised to play an increasing role in military systems. Thirty countries in the United Nations have explicitly endorsed the call for a ban on lethal autonomous weapons systems. It was noted in the corresponding open letter [60]: "We, the undersigned, call upon governments and government leaders to create a future with strong international norms, regulations, and laws against lethal autonomous weapons. These currently being absent, we opt to hold ourselves to a high standard: we will neither participate in nor support the development, manufacture, trade, or use of lethal autonomous weapons. We ask that technology companies and organizations, as well as leaders, policymakers, and other individuals, join us in this pledge". To date, this pledge has been signed by 3806 individuals and 274 organizations including Google DeepMind, the Montreal Institute for Learning Algorithms, Silicon Valley Robotics, The Swedish AI Society, the Italian Association for Artificial Intelligence, the European Association for Artificial Intelligence (EurAI) and others.

United Kingdom (Britain Bletchley Park, Buckinghamshire) hosted the world's largest artificial intelligence safety event, the AI Safety Summit [61], which was attended by representatives of 29 governments, including the US, Canada, China, European Union, Australia, Germany, Ukraine, and others. Participants signed the Bletchley Declaration on Artificial Intelligence [62], a document in which the governments of various countries agreed to join forces on AI security. Cooperation between the countries will focus on identifying AI risks and developing security policies based on these risks. First, it concerns such areas as cybersecurity, biotechnology, and disinformation.

US President Biden issued a landmark Executive Order [63] to ensure that America leads the way in seizing the promise and managing the risks of AI. The Executive Order establishes new standards for AI safety and security, protects Americans' privacy, advances equity and civil rights, stands up for consumers and workers, promotes innovation and competition, advances American leadership around the world, and more. The Executive Order builds on previous actions the President has taken, including work that led to voluntary commitments from 15 leading AI companies to drive safe, secure, and trustworthy development of AI.

Finally, the EU agreed a "historic" deal with the world's first laws to regulate AI. In particular, the Agreement between the European Parliament and member states [64, 65] will govern AI, social media, and search engines. The world's first comprehensive laws to regulate artificial intelligence have been agreed in a landmark deal after a marathon 37-hour negotiation between the European Parliament and EU member states. A suite of laws in Europe will also govern social media and search engines, covering giants such as X, TikTok and Google.

All the abovementioned underline that AI is a revolutionary technology that will influence all countries in the world, all domains of human activity, all people, and our planet as a whole. However, the implementation of advanced AI deals with corresponding risks, which can be decreased if all developers, designers, and creators of AI systems follow regulation laws and ethical rules in the field of AI with its human-centered application.

1.7 Conclusion

We reviewed the current landscape of global AI deployment, ethical concerns, advantages, challenges, disadvantages, and dangers of advanced AI implementation. National AI strategies and successful AI implementation in diverse fields affirm AI's transformative global significance. Analysis of AI's advantages and threats shows that it will have a strong influence on the job market and human activities.

The implementation peculiarities of AI are analyzed based on the 50 national strategies for AI development in developed countries, NATO official documents devoted to AI development for the period 2023–2043, and the

Ukrainian conception and project of strategy for AI development and implementations. Many examples are considered for demonstration of the positive and negative aspects of AI applications at the current stage and in the future. Advances in AI are at the heart of many of 2024's most exciting areas of technological innovation [66], including deep learning for protein design, deepfakes detection, large-fragment DNA insertion, brain–computer interfaces, super-duper resolution, cell atlases, and nanomaterials printed in 3D.

Special attention is paid to the international movement for creating regulation laws and moral-ethic norms and rules for AI development and implementation with discussion corresponding open letters on AI dangers and regulation, the Bletchley Declaration on Artificial Intelligence signed by representatives of 29 governments, the Executive Order on AI in the USA, agreement between the European Parliament and member states on laws to regulate AI and others.

AI must provide a happy future for humankind and this must be the main goal and main task for researchers, designers, and creators of advanced AI systems and technologies.

References

[1]   Y. Kondratenko, A. Shevchenko, Y. Zhukov, V. Slyusar, M. Klymenko, G. Kondratenko, O. Striuk, 'Analysis of the Priorities and Perspectives in Artificial Intelligence Implementation', 13th International IEEE Conference "Dependable Systems, Services and Technologies" (DESSERT'2023), Greece, Athens, October 13-15, 2023.

[2]   Y. Kondratenko, G. Kondratenko, A. Shevchenko, V. Slyusar, Y. Zhukov, M. Vakulenko, 'Towards Implementing the Strategy of Artificial Intelligence Development: Ukraine Peculiarities', CEUR Workshop Proceedings, vol. 3513, 2023, pp. 106-117, https://ceur-ws.org/Vol-3513/paper09.pdf.

[3]   Y. Kondratenko, A. Shevchenko, Y. Zhukov, G. Kondratenko, O. Striuk, 'Tendencies and Challenges of Artificial Intelligence Development and Implementation', Proceedings of the 12th IEEE International Conference on Intelligent Data Acquisition and Advanced Computing Systems: Technology and Applications, IDAACS'2023, Vol. 1, 2023, pp. 221 – 226, IDAACS 2023, Dortmund, Germany, 7-9 September 2023.

[4]   P. Lee, C. Golberg, I. Kohane, 'The AI revolution in medicine: GPT-4 and beyond', Pearson Education Inc., 2023.

[5]   Y. P. Kondratenko, N. Y. Kondratenko, 'Reduced library of the soft computing analytic models for arithmetic operations with asymmetrical fuzzy numbers', in: Soft Computing: Developments, Methods and

Applications, A. Casey (Ed), NOVA Science Publishers, Hauppauge, New York, 2016, pp. 1-38.

[6]   V. Slyusar, et al., 'Improvement of the object recognition model on aerophotos using deep conventional neural network', East. Eur. J. Enterp. Technol., Vol. 5, No. 2 (113), pp. 6-21, 2021.

[7]   D. Chumachenko, et al., 'Machine Learning Methods in Predicting Patients with Suspected Myocardial Infarction Based on Short-Time HRV Data', Sensors, vol. 22, no. 18, 7033, 2022.

[8]   A. Hanna, E. Bender, 'AI Hurts Consumers and Workers and Isn't Intelligent', TechPolicy Press, August 4, 2023.

[9]   '50 National AI Strategies - The 2020 AI Strategy Landscape', https://bit.ly/3DByraQ.

[10]   'The Global AI Strategy Landscape', https://bit.ly/3LFvGY9.

[11]   T. Kohli, 'AI's contribution to the global economy will bypass that of China and India by 2030, to reach $15.7 trillion', World Economic Forum, September 17, 2019, https://www.weforum.org/agenda/2019/09/artificial-intelligence-mee tsbiotechnology/.

[12]   'Ukrainian developers use artificial intelligence for more accurate drone bombardment', 2022, https://bit.ly/3f1bZh3.

[13]   V. Slyusar, N. Hamaliy, 'New model of NATO defense planning process, NDPP', Coordination problems of military-technical and defensive industrial policy in Ukraine. Weapons and military equipment development perspectives, V International Scientific and Practical Conference, Abstracts of reports, Kyiv, 11-12 October 2017, pp. 38-39.

[14]   Z. Stanley-Lockman, E. H. Christis, 'An Artificial Intelligence Strategy for NATO', NATO, October 2021.

[15]   'NATO starts work on Artificial Intelligence certification standard', 07 February 2023, https://www.nato.int/cps/en/natohq/news_211498.htm.

[16]   D.F. Reding, et al., 'Science & Technology Trends 2023-2043', vol. 1-2, NATO Science and Technology Organization, Brussels, Belgium, March 2023.

[17]   'Summary of NATO's Quantum Technologies Strategy', 16 January 2024, https://www.nato.int/cps/en/natohq/official_texts_221777.htm.

[18]   'AFRL. Artificial Intelligence – Air Force Research Laboratory', 2022, https://afresearchlab.com/technology/artificial-intelligence/(visitedon12/30/2023).

[19]   V. Slyusar, 'Reducing the Cognitive Burden of a Soldier with the Help of a Personal AI and LLM Assistant', Human Systems Integration Team of Experts (HSI ToE) Virtual Winter Symposium, 12 January 2024, DOI: 10.13140/RG.2.2.10264.57605/1.

[20]   M. Klymkovetsky, 'NATO scientists will help Ukrainian developers in the field of military innovations', 26 May 2023, https://hromadske.ua/posts/naukovci-nato-dopomagatimut-ukrayinskim-rozrobnikam-u-sferi-vijskovih-innovacij-mincifri

[21] 'On the Approval of the Concept of Artificial Intelligence Development in Ukraine', bit.ly/44GrVKh

[22] Shevchenko, A. I., et al., 'Regarding the Draft Strategy Development of Artificial Intelligence in Ukraine (2022 – 2030)', Artificial Intelligence (Shtuchnyi Intelekt), No. 1, pp. 8-157, 2022.

[23] Shevchenko, A.I., et al. 'Strategy for Artificial Intelligence Development in Ukraine', Monograph, IAIP, Kyiv, 2023, DOI:10.15407/development_strategy_2 023.

[24] Y. Kondratenko, I. Atamanyuk, I. Sidenko, G. Kondratenko, S. Sichevskyi, 'Machine Learning Techniques for Increasing Efficiency of the Robot's Sensor and Control Information Processing', Sensors, vol. 22, no. 3, 1062, January 2022.

[25] 'Engineers from Ukraine presented a radar-invisible electric unmanned submarine Kronos', BuildingTECH, 23 February 2023.

[26] J. Hudson, K. Khudov, 'The war in Ukraine is spurring a revolution in drone warfare using AI', The Washington Post, 26 July, 2023, https://www.wa shingtonpost.com/world/2023/07/26/drones-ai-ukraine-war-innovation/

[27] 'Ukrainian kamikaze robot Ratel S launched into mass production. 24 October 2023, https://news.pn/ru/RussiaInvadedUkraine/299190

[28] R. Duro, Y. Kondratenko (eds), Advances in Intelligent Robotics and Collaborative Automation, River Publishers, Aalborg, 2015.

[29] Y. P. Kondratenko, L. P. Klymenko, V. Y. Kondratenko, G. V. Kondratenko, E. A. Shvets, 'Slip displacement sensors for intelligent robots: Solutions and models', Proceedings of the 2013 IEEE 7th International Conference on Intelligent Data Acquisition and Advanced Computing Systems, IDAACS 2013, 2, art. no. 6663050, pp. 861-866, 2013, doi:10.1109/IDAACS.2 013.6663050

[30] V. M. Kuntsevich, V. F. Gubarev, Y. P. Kondratenko, D. V. Lebedev, and V. P. Lysenko (Eds.), 'Control Systems: Theory and Applications', River Publishers, Girsrup, Delft, 2018.

[31] 'Ukrzaliznytsia: Processing passenger requests using ChatGPT', https://ww w.facebook.com/Ukrzaliznytsia/posts/pfbid033VCGWzXrCDvkcrP221opg79sPsGG8BLDQivk87q HfSrW1h667u2TCRQPKHn28sNil

[32] 'Fedorov stated that Ukraine has started work on a strategy for regulating artificial intelligence', 3 August 2023, https://news.pn/ru/public/ 295074

[33] 'Dmytro Lubinets: artificial intelligence is used to search for missing people', 16 November 2023, https://ombudsman.gov.ua/news_details/dmitro-lubi nec-shtuchnij-intelekt-vikoristovuyut-dlya-poshuku-zniklih-bezvisti-lyudej

[34] V. Kolomiyets, 'Artificial intelligence will help to check the declarations of officials', Hromadske, 22 December 2023, https://hromadske.ua/posts/shtuchn ij-intelekt-dopomozhe-pereviryati-deklaraciyi-chinovnikiv-nazk

[35] A. I. Shevchenko, M. S. Klymenko, 'Developing a Model of Artificial Conscience', in: 15th IEEE International Scientific and Technical Conference on Computer Sciences and Information Technologies, CSIT'2020, vol. 1, 23-26 Sept. 2020, Lviv-Zbarazh, pp. 51–54, 2020.

[36] E. Hildt, 'Artificial Intelligence: Does Consciousness Matter?', Front. Psychology 10, 2019.

[37] R. Manzotti, A. Chella, 'Good Old-Fashioned Artificial Consciousness and the Intermediate Level Fallacy', Frontiers in Robotics and AI 5, 2018.

[38] A. I. Shevchenko, 'Natural Human Intelligence - The Object of Research for Artificial Intelligence Creation', International Scientific and Technical Conference on Computer Sciences and Information Technologies, 2019, 1, pp. XXVI–XXIX, 8929799, CSIT 2019, Lviv, 17-20 September 2019.

[39] L. Medeiros, D. Psaltis, T. R. Lauer, F. Özel, 'The Image of the M87 Black Hole Reconstructed with PRIMO', The Astrophysical Journal Letters, 947:L7 (6pp), 10 April 2023, https://iopscience.iop.org/article/10.3847/2041-8213/acc32d/pdf

[40] O. Struik, Y. Kondratenko, 'Optimization Strategy for Generative Adversarial Networks Design', International Journal of Computing, vol. 22(3), pp. 292–301, 2023. DOI:10.47839/ijc.22.3.3223

[41] O. Struik, Y. Kondratenko, 'Implementation of Generative Adversarial Networks in Mobile Applications for Image Data Enhancement', Journal of Mobile Multimedia, 19(3), pp. 823–838, 2023.

[42] O. Struik, Y. Kondratenko, 'Generative Adversarial Neural Networks and Deep Learning: Successful Cases and Advanced Approaches', International Journal of Computing, Vol. 20, Issue 3, pp. 339-349, 2021.

[43] P. Scharre, 'AI's inhuman advantage', Texas National Security Reviw, 10 April 2023, https://warontherocks.com/2023/04/ais-inhuman-advantage/

[44] 'French Open 2023: Grand Slam using AI to protect players from online abuse', BBC, 28 May 2023, https://www.bbc.com/sport/tennis/65706479

[45] 'Japan is introducing technology to recognize drivers' emotions using AI to improve road safety', https://news.pn/uk/public/294347

[46] A. Taylor, 'Albania to speed up EU accession using ChatGPT', EURACTIV, 12 December 2023, https://www.euractiv.com/section/politics/news/albania-to-speed-up-eu-accession-using-chatgpt/

[47] R. Browne, 'An AI just negotiated a contract for the first time ever — and no human was involved', CNBC, 12 November 2023, https://www.cnbc.com/2023/11/07/ai-negotiates-legal-contract-without-humans-involved-for-first-time.html

[48] D. Trotta, 'California turns to AI to help spot wildfires', Reuters, 11 August 2023, https://www.reuters.com/world/us/california-turns-ai-help-spot-wildfires-2023-08-11/

[49] 'UK cybersecurity center says 'deepfakes' and other AI tools pose a threat to the next election', AP, 14 November 2023, https://apnews.com/art icle/uk-cyber-threats-ai-elections-b6482d3127ae524551e15887b3fdb01b

[50] P. Glynn, 'Sony World Photography Award 2023: Winner refuses award after revealing AI creation', BBC, 18 April 2023, https://www.bbc.com/news/ent ertainment-arts-65296763

[51] A. Crawford, T. Smith, 'Illegal trade in AI child sex abuse images exposed', BBC, 28 June 2023, https://www.bbc.com/news/uk-65932372

[52] 'In South Korea, an industrial robot mistakenly killed a man', https://news .pn/uk/public/299999

[53] M. Sellman, 'ChatGPT falsely accuses law professor of sex assault', The Times, 6 April 2023, https://www.thetimes.co.uk/article/chatgpt-falsely-accuses-law-profe ssor-of-sex-assault-fmvfhptpp?fbclid=IwAR2Ixhwr5-ezAgr8wCICZiCj2yN6uwST4x7yDbKOvl2R P5Qf9XN44Nrn6Uc

[54] D. Baschuk, 'Tech, AI Driving Job Changes for Nearly a Quarter of All Workers', Bloomberg, 30 April 2023, https://www.bloomberg.com/news/articles/2023 -04-30/tech-ai-driving-job-changes-for-nearly-a-quarter-of-all-workers?srnd=premium-europe &leadSource=uverify%20wall

[55] J. Henley, 'German tabloid Bild cuts 200 jobs and says some roles will be replaced by AI', The Guardian, 20 June 2023, https://www.theguardian.com/worl d/2023/jun/20/german-tabloid-bild-to-replace-range-of-editorial-jobs-with-ai

[56] P. Gmyrek, J. Berg, D. Bescond, 'Generative AI and jobs: A global analysis of potential effects on job quantity and quality', International Labor Organization, ILO Working Paper 96, August 2023, https://www.ilo.org/wc msp5/groups/public/---dgreports/---inst/documents/publication/wcms_890761.pdf

[57] S. Russell, 'AI weapons: Russia's war in Ukraine shows why the world must enact a ban', Nature, v. 614, pp. 620-623, 23 February 2023.

[58] Z. Kleinman, C. Vallance, 'AI 'godfather' Geoffrey Hinton warns of dangers as he quits Google', BBC, 2 May 2023, https://www.bbc.com/news/w orld-us-canada-65452940

[59] 'Pause Giant AI Experiments: An Open Letter', Future of Life Institute, 22 March 2023, https://futureoflife.org/open-letter/pause-giant-ai-experiments/

[60] 'Lethal Autonomous Weapons Pledge. An Open Letter', Future of Life Institute, 6 June 2023, https://futureoflife.org/open-letter/lethal-autonomous-weapons-p ledge/

[61] 'Ukraine has signed an international declaration dedicated to the safety of the use of AI', 2 November 2023, https://thedigital.gov.ua/news/ukraina-pidpisala -mizhnarodnu-deklaratsiyu-prisvyachenu-bezpetsi-vikoristannya-shi

[62] 'The Bletchley Declaration by Countries Attending the AI Safety Summit', 1-2 November 2023, https://www.gov.uk/government/publications/ai-sa fety-summit-2023-the-bletchley-declaration/the-bletchley-declaration-by-countries-attending- the-ai-safety-summit-1-2-november-2023

[63]   'Fact Sheet: President Bidcn Issues Executive Order on Safe, Secure, and Trustworthy Artificial Intelligence', White House, 30 October 2023, https://www.whitehouse.gov/briefing-room/statements-releases/2023/10/30/fact-sheet-president-biden-issues-executive-order-on-safe-secure-and-trustworthy-artificial-intelligence/

[64]   L. O'Carroll, 'EU agrees 'historic' deal with world's first laws to regulate AI', The Gardian, 8 December 2023, https://www.theguardian.com/world/2023/dec/08/eu-agrees-historic-deal-with-worlds-first-laws-to-regulate-ai

[65]   Ye. Gubina, 'The European Union has taken an important step towards the regulation of artificial intelligence', Meza, 15 June 2023. https://mezha.media/2023/06/15/yevrosoiuz-zrobyv-vazhlyvyy-krok/

[66]   M. Eisenstein, 'Seven technologies to watch in 2024', Nature, Vol 625, pp. 844-848, 25 January 2024.

Authors' Short CV

Anatolii Shevchenko graduated from the Faculty of Physics at Donetsk State University with a major in Radio Physics and Electronics. In 1985, he defended his Ph.D. thesis, earning the academic degree of a candidate. In 1990, he completed his doctoral thesis, obtaining the academic degree of Doctor of Technical Sciences. In 1997, he was awarded the title of professor, and in 1998, he received the honorary title of Honored Scientist and Technician of Ukraine. In 2006, was elected as a Corresponding Member of the National Academy of Sciences of Ukraine in the field of Computer Systems. In 2015, he was appointed as the Director of the Institute of Artificial Intelligence of the Ministry of Education and Science of Ukraine and the National Academy of Sciences of Ukraine in Kyiv. Together with the Department of Informatics of the National Academy of Sciences of Ukraine, he initiated an international scientific journal called "Artificial Intelligence" and was appointed as its chief editor. His research interests encompass various aspects of artificial intelligence, modelling human intelligence, simulating elements of human consciousness, breakthrough technologies in the field of artificial intelligence, and multidisciplinary aspects of artificial intelligence.

Yuriy Kondratenko is a Doctor of Science, Professor, Honour Inventor of Ukraine (2008), Corr. Academician of Royal Academy of Doctors (Barcelona, Spain), Head of the Department of Intelligent Information Systems at Petro Mohyla Black Sea National University (PMBSNU), Ukraine, Leading Researcher of the Institute of Artificial Intelligence Problems of MES and NAS of Ukraine, Fulbright Scholar. He received a Ph.D. (1983) and Dr.Sc. (1994) at Odessa National Polytechnic University, and several international grants and scholarships for conducting research in P.R. of China, Germany, and the USA. Research interests include robotics, automation, sensors and control systems, intelligent decision support systems, and fuzzy logic.

Vadym Slyusar is a Doctor of Science, Professor, Honoured Scientist and Technician of Ukraine (2008). He received a Ph.D. in 1992, Doctor of Sciences in 2000, and Professor in 2005. His research interests include radar systems, smart antennas for wireless communications and digital beamforming, artificial intelligence, and robotics.

Igor Atamanyuk is a Professor, Doctor of Science (habilt.) and Professor of the Department of Applied Mathematics at Warsaw University of Life Sciences, Poland. He is a specialist in in the theory of random processes, math statistics, operations research, cybernetics and applied mathematics. His research interests include modeling, recognition, filtering and forecasting of random processes, decision-making, and computer control systems.

Galyna Kondratenko is an Associate Professor, Ph.D., Associate Professor of the Intelligent Information Systems Department at Petro Mohyla Black Sea National University, Ukraine. She is a specialist in control systems, decision-making, and fuzzy logic. She worked in the framework of international scientific university cooperation during the implementation of international projects with the European Union: TEMPUS (Cabriolet), Erasmus + (Aliot) and DAAD-Ostpartnerschaftsprogramm (projects with the University of Saarland, Germany). Her research interests include computer control systems, fuzzy logic, decision-making, and intelligent robotic devices.

Tetiana Yeroshenko obtained her Ph.D. degree in 2016 in the field of Philosophy of Science from the H.S. Skovoroda Institute of Philosophy (Kyiv, Ukraine). She is a research scientist at the Department of Theoretical Research in the field of artificial intelligence at the Institute of Artificial Intelligence of the Ministry of Education and Science of Ukraine and the National Academy of Sciences of Ukraine (Kyiv). Her research interests include the philosophy of science and multidisciplinary aspects of artificial intelligence.

Interrelation and Inter-influence of Artificial Intelligence and Higher Education Systems

Y. P. Kondratenko[1,2], V. I. Slyusar[1,*], M. B. Solesvik[3], N. Y. Kondratenko[4], and Z. Gomolka[5]

[1]Institute of Artificial Intelligence Problems of MES and NAS of Ukraine, Kyiv, Ukraine
[2]Intelligent Information Systems Department, Petro Mohyla Black Sea National University, Mykolaiv, Ukraine
[3]Western Norway University of Applied Sciences, Bergen, Norway
[4]Darla Moore School of Business, University of South Carolina, Columbia, SC, United States of America
[5]Department of Computer Engineering, University of Rzeszow, Rzeszow, Poland
E-mail: y_kondrat2002@yahoo.com, swadim@ukr.net, marina.solesvik@hvl.no, nina.kondratenko@grad.moore.sc.edu, zgomolka@ur.edu.pl
[*]Corresponding Author

Abstract

Artificial intelligence (AI) will make revolutionary transformations in different areas of human activity. This chapter is devoted to the current state and perspectives of AI implementation in the education sphere. The potential possibilities and proposals for AI use in research, learning, and teaching processes are discussed, with illustrations of the successful cases. Special attention is paid to (a) the interrelation and interconnection of AI and higher education systems and (b) to improving qualified cadre training in the AI field based on education in the framework of specialized AI consortia that united universities/colleges and advanced AI companies. Some examples of AI educational consortia existing in different countries and continents confirm the efficiency of the consortia approach for strengthening research, learning, and teaching processes.

Keywords: Artificial intelligence; education; implementation; interrelation; academic consortia.

2.1 Introduction

Methods and tools of artificial intelligence (AI) have been widely introduced to different fields of human activity, including medicine, transport, climate science, communication, and industry [1, 2, 3, 4, 5, 6]. At the same time, special attention should be paid to the education sphere, in particular, (a) to training AI specialists who will design perspective AI systems and (b) to introducing advanced AI technologies in learning and teaching processes to increase the efficiency of graduates' preparation in different domains (device-, machine- and ship-building, agriculture, civil construction, medicine, social work, public administration, and others). The human–AI collaboration in decision-making processes plays an important role in the successful application of advanced AI tools and systems [7, 8].

The governments of many developed countries have ambitious goals to be on the front line of AI development and implementation in the world and they understand that these ambitions may be realized only through the development of young talents and efficient cadres' preparation in modern AI technologies.

So, on the one hand, the efficiency of the AI systems now and in the future depends on the high qualification skills, moral-ethical principles, and mentality of the AI designers and creators. Many discussions are now taking place between scientists and policymakers about the risks of AI implementation for people, ecology, and the environment, taking into account the potential challenges and dangers of such implementation. At the same time, the behavior of AI systems corresponds to the conceptions, algorithms, theories, methods, and different innovations applied by AI creators in design processes [9–12]. According to Demis Hassabis's (DeepMind CEO) opinion [13], AI behavior is as good as its designer (creator).

On the other hand, AI tools and systems can help prepare AI specialists at universities with high skills in machine learning, deep learning, pattern recognition, computer vision, biocomputing, fuzzy logic, quantum computing, and other AI-related disciplines. Such graduates can become members of leading AI design companies and can influence the features, properties, and peculiarities of future AI design and implementation processes. Indeed, strong interrelation and inter-influence exist between AI and higher education systems.

Large language models and generative AI need to be applied such that their potential to harm does not outweigh their benefits [14]. It seems that such systems will need to be regulated by globally coordinated agreements, like for such innovations as nuclear materials, drugs, and vaccines. It is impossible to predict precisely the impact of these AI technologies and innovations for the next 100 years but, no doubt, the world and people's lives will be significantly changed. That is why it is necessary to continue coordinating regulatory policy for AI technologies to create disruptive innovations that are more useful than harmful for humans, economies, and the environment.

The main goal of this chapter is an analysis of the main perspectives of AI implementation in higher education, a discussion of the AI and academic processes (learning and teaching) interconnections, as well as successful cases and important ways and approaches for increasing the efficiency of the preparation of high-caliber specialists in the AI field.

The rest of the chapter is presented in the following way. Section 2 discusses the priorities in ChatGPT and other large language model implementations to education activities. The successful cases of AI development and application in higher education institutions are considered in Section 3. Section 4 is devoted to the analysis of the advantages of AI implementation for students, teachers, and researchers in the framework of academic and academia/AI-company consortia. Section 5 includes the conclusions and description of future research.

2.2 Priority Approaches of the Implementation of ChatGPT and Similar LLMs in Learning, Teaching and Research

The US technological company OpenAI from San Francisco, California presented its AI chatbot ChatGPT on 30 November 2022. Since this date, ChatGPT has become one of the most popular large language models (LLMs), which can help people to get a piece of advice or to solve routing and even creative tasks in a "question–answer" dialog mode. One million people in the first 5 days were registered as ChatGPT users and after about one year the number of users increased to more than 180 million [15].

Special attention should be paid to the introduction of LLM ChatGPT and its derivatives for academic and scientific purposes, in particular for increasing the efficiency of learning, teaching, and research processes. Many successful cases are discussed in the latest publications concerning the interrelation between AI and higher educational systems [15, 16, 17, 18]. The versions of ChatGPT, such as GPT-3, GPT-3.5, and GPT-4v can be easily reached using Internet resources on a non-fee and fee-paid basis. The properties, possibilities, and characteristics of such LLMs are constantly increasing and improving due to the development and increasing number of embedded plugins (more than 1000).

Some interesting discussions about the promise and perils of AI in academia are reflected in, for example, the journal Nature [15], open lectures [19], and international scientific conferences and workshops [2, 3, 4].

The recent rise of generative artificial intelligence has created unprecedented opportunities and challenges for academics. Driven by economic incentives, the pace at which artificial intelligence is evolving is staggering, with transformative changes in education and research to be expected.

While preliminary guidelines have been set forth by universities, the swift progress in the field of artificial intelligence will require ongoing evaluation. While most universities support the careful use of those tools [19], the University of Hong Kong announced that it would fully embrace the use of generative AI.

New York City Public Schools [20] also are determined to embrace ChatGPT's potential in learning and teaching processes and students will be taught how to use AI.

Elementary and middle schools in Seoul are set to introduce robots for one-on-one English-speaking programs next academic year [21]. The "English tutor robot" is an AI-installed robot that will be capable of communicating with students in English, as well as offering customized one-on-one learning. The education office will also pilot a chatbot app that enables students to engage in a conversation with the software based on a topic selected by the user. An existing exchange program connecting South Korean students with students overseas through translation and interpretation software will expand seriously by 2026.

The Ministry of Digital Transformation of Ukraine, together with the technology company Google [22], launched a free course on artificial intelligence "Basics of AI" for Ukrainians in May–June 2023. Google noted that the program is built according to the principle from simple to more complex. Among the main topics of the course are: (a) what is AI and why is it needed; (b) which ready-made AI-based solutions can be used in various areas – from marketing to facility management; (c) ML (machine learning) implementation strategy in the company; (d) nuances of building a technical team to work with ML; (e) how to apply ready-made ML solutions without coding experience.

The Ministry of Education and Science (MES) of Ukraine has launched a test based on artificial intelligence, which can help students determine their future profession [23]. A unique tool of the project, which can be used by every student free of charge, is career guidance testing based on artificial intelligence. The MES added that such testing helps teenagers "accurately and quickly" determine their inclination to more than 1000 professions, learn about new, relevant, and promising types of activities, as well as understand how successful the choice of a certain profession will be in the future.

The COVID-19 pandemic has ushered the education system into a tech-savvy path. The Ministry of Human Resources and Development, Government of India has proposed a draft of the National Education Policy (NEP) [24] where the focus is on enhancing teaching and learning through an online mode. In the NEP, universities and higher education institutions are directed to dedicate a budget for online EdTechs (such as LMS, Moodle, Microsoft Teams, Google Suite, etc.). The policy also emphasizes promoting teaching through advanced technological tools such as artificial intelligence, big data, virtual reality, 3D printing and robotics, developing technical infrastructure, and supporting the advanced teaching and learning mechanism.

Lucas Wesemann [19] discusses practical use cases and the corresponding risks of AI in academia, including its role in hyper-personalized learning, literature reviews, coding, laboratory setups, academic writing, assisting non-native English speakers, grant proposals, AI-assisted peer-review and publication, and its capability to support the development of new research hypotheses and ideas. The main goal of many AI scientists is to inspire discussions on the safe and productive use of AI in academia.

The main approaches for LLMs ChatGPT and GPT-4 implementation in the education sphere are presented in Table 2.1, which are formulated based on the authors' proposals and existing successful experiences [2, 3, 4, 18, 25–34] in the completely academic community.

LLMs are typically trained using huge amounts of text, or other information, which they use to generate realistic answers by predicting what comes next

Table 2.1: The AI abilities for implementation in research, learning and teaching

Process (users)	LLM's role	Approach (proposal), function
Learning (students, distance-learning students)	Personal tutor (based on plugins Tutory, EdX, OpenLecture, Giga Tutor and others)	To form a personalized and flexible learning environment.
		To explain physical laws, concepts, or different scientific ideas.
		To evaluate the current level of understanding of the learning material by students and form specialized exercises for knowledge improvement.
Learning (groups of students)	Group tutor	Coordinate group projects for collaborative learning, creating an environment for discussion, and providing feedback on group dynamics.
		Generate dynamic simulations or scenarios that allow students to apply their knowledge in a virtual environment.
Learning (students with disabilities)	Personal assistant	To convert text to speech for students with visual disabilities, etc.
		To provide simplified explanations for students with cognitive disabilities.
Learning (foreign and native students)	Multi-language tutor (using plugins Speak and Speechki)	To help with the creation of multilingual learning resources and provide access to education based on different languages.
		To help in learning native and foreign languages, providing instant feedback on grammar, pronunciation, and vocabulary.
		To provide real-time translation services for students who speak different languages.
Learning (students)	Personal assistant	To help in navigation in the learning process.
		To advise on choosing courses, career paths, and personal development programs.
Learning (students)	Personal consultant	To provide 24/7 dialogue based on students' own schedules and personal learning pace.
		To form answers to students' questions.
		To conduct seminars and discussions.
		To help students understand how AI systems work and analyze the moral-ethical aspects of their implementation.

Table 2.1: Continued.

Process (users)	LLM's role	Approach (proposal), function
Learning: medical aspects (students)	Emotional supporter	To help students cope with stress and maintain mental health.
		To help in developing mindfulness exercises, stress management techniques, or providing compassionate communication.
		Identify the situations where a student is experiencing emotional difficulties and suggest appropriate resources or interventions.
Teaching (teachers)	Assistant/ consultant	To help in automatically grading assignments or creating learning content.
		To generate lecture summaries, self-test questions, interactive practice exercises, quizzes, lesson plans, examples, and scenarios to illustrate complex topics and so on.
		To help in the review process for students' control and homework.
		To recognize plagiarism or inconsistencies in the students' manuscripts.
		To develop suggestions for improving the clarity and coherence of written texts.
		To help with the evaluation of the assignments, organizing feedback for students, and recognizing topics where students are struggling and need additional consultations or explanation support.
		To provide additional information resources for professional development.
		To form proposals for improving teaching strategies and fresh information about the latest achievements and advances in the corresponding subjects or research domains.
Academic management (university managers)	Assistant/ consultant	The effective management of the resources of educational institutions, the management of library resources, or the coordination of services for students.
		To help in the optimal distribution of the academic load among teachers.
		To help in the preparation of lesson schedules at the institute or university level.

Table 2.1: Continued.

Process (users)	LLM's role	Approach (proposal), function
		To support decision-making processes in typical and non-standard situations of managerial activity.
Research (researchers)	Scientific assistant	To help in providing quick access to information, generating ideas for research and writing or correcting fragments of scientific reports, dissertations, or articles, summarizing large volumes of text, identifying key themes in the literature, and even suggesting areas for further research.
		To help with data analysis and symbolic computation based on the Wolfram plugin.

[16]. As usual, the bigger the model is the better it performs. Modern LLMs have more than one hundred billion adjustable parameters. Some researchers predict that modern LLMs as AI tools will eventually achieve artificial general intelligence (AGI), matching and even exceeding humans in solving most tasks.

In particular, the game Set has long inspired mathematicians to create interesting tasks such as optimization problems. Today, the LLM-based approach shows that AI can help mathematicians to generate new efficient solutions [17]. FunSearch (as an AI system) made progress on Set-inspired problems in combinatorics, a field of mathematics that studies how to count the possible arrangements of sets containing finitely many objects. Mathematical chatbot FunSearch automatically creates requests for a specially trained LLM, asking the LLM to write short computer programs for generating solutions to a particular mathematical problem. Then LLM rapidly compares the obtained solutions with known existing variants and provides feedback to the LLM for improving solutions in the next round.

Scientists also use LLMs for the preparation of the applications for research grants but they should exercise caution in such cases because AI-generated text might not be meaningful. AI is not founded on a deep knowledge of the context of the scientific problem, the research gap, the broader societal impact, the ethical responsibilities involved, and the researcher's values [35]. Researchers can delegate their writing to ChatGPT to the extent that they take intellectual ownership and ethical responsibility for its words. However, they must think critically about when, how and why to use generative AI in light of the communicative context, audience needs, medium and purpose of writing. A critically literate approach to AI invites scientists to use generative AI to assist scientific communication, not substitute for it.

AI abilities allow the formation of the science policy but such policy should be based on judgments [36] because the role of judgments and ethical values in scientific research is very important. The black-box nature of AI makes it less transparent in the decision-making processes, in particular when using AI methods for science policy advice. In some cases, there is a risk that governments will claim to "follow AI" when developing policies that should be based openly on judgments, scientific evidence, and expert advice.

On the other hand, an important trend now is also the rapid development of small language models (SLMs). Depending on quantization level, SLMs have sizes in the range from 3 GB to 95 MB. This allows you to use them as a personal assistant in smartphones and even smartwatches. At the same time, their capabilities far exceed the functionality of LLMs of previous architectures. Technical aspects of the integration of the SLM Gemini Nano small speech model in a smartphone, general cases of its use, and the main advantages of using such a system in a smartphone in the future are given in [37].

As an alternative to the proprietary Gemini Nano, a variety of free SLM versions should be considered, including the Walter-StableLM-3B. Its general characteristics are given in Table 2.2 [38]. An alternative to this SLM is StableLM-Zephyr-3B [38], the characteristics of which, in particular the size and general requirements for the use of RAM, are somewhat similar. Based on the MT-Bench chart (Figure 2.1, [38]), StableLM-Zephyr-3B has a balanced performance across multiple tasks, with particularly strong results in areas like humanities, writing, roleplay, reasoning, and STEM-related tasks. This suggests that it is well-suited for applications that require a blend of creative and

Table 2.2: Sizes of the Walter-StableLM-3B versions.

Name	Quantization method	Size
walter-stablelm-3b.q2_k.gguf	Q2_k	1.20 GB
walter-stablelm-3b.q3_k_m.gguf	Q3_k_m	1.39 GB
walter-stablelm-3b.q4_k_m.gguf	Q4_k_m	1.71 GB
walter-stablelm-3b.q5_k_m.gguf	Q5_k_m	1.99 GB
walter-stablelm-3b.q6_k.gguf	Q6_k	2.30 GB
walter-stablelm-3b.q8_k.gguf	Q8_k	2.97 GB
walter-stablelm-3b.fp16.gguf	Fp16	5.59 GB

Figure 2.1: The MT-Bench chart compares the performance of LLM StableLM-Zephyr-3B across various tasks

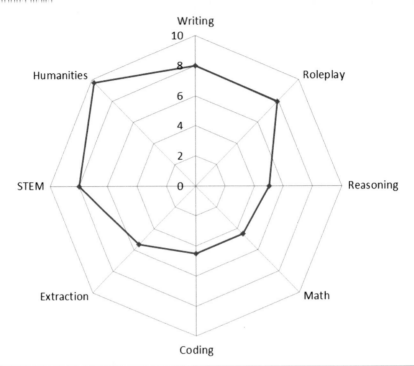

analytical thinking, such as technical writing or problem-solving in scientific contexts. Its robust performance indicates it could be reliable for a wide range of tasks, which may include language translation. The model's versatility makes it a potentially valuable tool for professionals and researchers who need assistance with complex language and problem-solving tasks.

On the other hand, the MT-Bench chart indicates that the StableLM-Zephyr-3B might have relative disadvantages in areas such as math, coding, and extraction. This could imply that the model may not be as proficient in understanding and generating mathematical explanations or coding that requires a deep grasp of nuances, and creativity.

TinyMistral-248M, Zephyr-220m, and Small_Llama-220M are representatives of the record holders, which have a very small size. For example, with 2-bit quantization, they can reach minimum sizes of 115 MB or 94.4 MB. This is enough to implement them as SLMs not only on smartphones but also on smartwatches.

Besides small text-oriented local LLMs, compact versions of multi-modal LLMs also deserve attention, particularly LLaVA (Large Language and Vision Assistant). They enable working with images, for instance, generating text reports based on created presentation slides, etc. The world's smallest multi-modal LLM in size, 3B, became Obsidian-3B. When quantized to a 6-bit representation of weight coefficients, its size is only 2.30 GB, whereas the Full Precision FP16 format of Obsidian-f16.gguf reaches 5.59 GB. An example of the application of the 6-bit version of Obsidian-q6.gguf for image description is shown in Figure 2.2.

Overall, the use of SLM on smart devices will contribute to the democratization of AI, making advanced AI technologies more accessible to the public. This will also lead to increased trust in such systems, will reduce their cost, and in the context of educational processes will allow expanding the scope of use of personal assistants for students beyond the limits indicated in Table 2.1.

Based on SLM, it is possible to create small versions of large action models (LAMs) as well, the first examples of which were presented at the CES2024

Figure 2.2: The result of using Obsidian-3B-V0.5-GGUF (obtained in the LM Studio application; the polar bear image is created in GPT-4o).

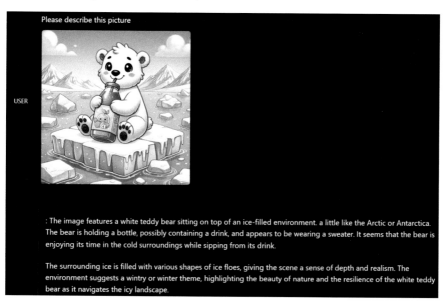

exhibition [39]. LAMs open a new direction in the development of interactive and responsive assistants based on AI, capable of adaptively performing tasks by understanding and reproducing human actions in digital environments. Unlike traditional LLMs focused on understanding and generating language, LAMs combine neuro-symbolic programming to understand the multimodal context and perform actions directly in applications. Considering the capabilities of LAMs, they can help students automate the management of the educational process based on project management technologies, organize their study materials, plan a study schedule, and assess progress in knowledge assimilation, interacting directly with educational platforms.

The innovation of LAM technology will provide more interactive simulations or synthetic laboratory environments (Figure 2.3), allowing students to conduct experiments virtually, thanks to the understanding and reproduction of human actions in mixed reality.

In this context, the concept of using LAMs to control student avatars in virtual experiments is proposed. In such a scenario, LAMs could interpret and translate students' commands or intentions into actions performed by avatars in a virtual environment. As an example, consider a prompt for a LAM to control avatars in a virtual chemical laboratory experiment:

"Initialize the virtual laboratory environment with the necessary equipment and materials for a titration experiment. Listen to students' commands using voice or text input. Interpret the students' instructions related to the experiment, such as 'take a test tube, fill it with acid, adjust the pH meter, and record observations.' Transform these instructions into avatar actions in the virtual environment, ensuring accurate and realistic movements and interaction.

Provide real-time feedback to students based on their actions, for instance, notify them if the test tube is overfilled or if the pH reading is stable. In the event of an emergency situation, such as the threat of virtual liquid spilling over the top of the test tube during heating – give the command to the avatar to press the electricity off button on the virtual heating device.

Allow collaborative interaction of several student avatars who need to work together and communicate in the virtual space.

At the end of the experiment, guide students through the process of virtual cleaning and safely dispose of any virtual chemicals. Provide a summary of the experiment results and suggest areas for improvement or further exploration."

The implementation of the described concept would represent a significant advancement in educational technologies, especially in fields that require

Figure 2.3: A virtual laboratory with students' avatars engaging in scientific exploration (DALL-E3).

practical experience or laboratory work. This would enable students to conduct experiments or participate in simulations that might be too dangerous, expensive, or impractical to perform in the real world. Such an approach would provide a more immersive and interactive learning experience, as students could directly manipulate their environment through their own avatars. Moreover, this application could be particularly beneficial in remote learning situations, where students do not have access to physical laboratories or equipment. By using LAM to control avatars, students could gain practical experience and develop skills that are otherwise hard to acquire through traditional online learning methods. This approach could also lead to new forms of collaborative learning, where students from different geographical locations work together in the same virtual space, controlling their avatars to conduct experiments and solve problems collectively. This would not only enhance the learning experience but also foster teamwork and communication skills. Therefore, it should be noted that using LAM to control avatars in virtual educational environments could revolutionize the way practical skills are taught and learned, making education more accessible, interactive, and effective.

LAMs can also automate routine data entry tasks, report document formatting, or experiment planning. With a direct interface to databases and research tools, LAMs can simplify the research process, helping students gather and organize information more efficiently.

Adaptive assistants based on LAM personalize educational content and its delivery methods according to the learning styles and preferences of individual students. They can take on the functions of organizing and conducting group meetings, conferences, and seminars, taking into account unpredictable changes in the scenario or program of the event. All this should free up time for students so they can focus on receiving positive emotions from learning and discovering new things.

2.3 Successful Cases of ChatGPT Application for Learning and Teaching Processes

Let us reflect on the successful cases of AI development and implementation for increasing the efficiency of the learning, teaching, and research processes. For example, Siddharth Kankaria [11] wrote about his positive experience of using CharGPT by himself and his students while teaching a course on Science Communication and Public Engagement. The teacher designed his sessions in a participatory and interactive style and used improvisation games, performances, debates and discussions to teach students the fundamental basis of science communication. The teacher used ChatGPT to brainstorm prompts, questions and content for student activities. At the same time, students were also invited to use ChatGPT to solve different tasks in the classroom. It was possible for the teacher and students together discuss the ChatGPT results, in particular, on science writing, discussing and criticizing together an anonymized mix of summaries of research papers written by ChatGPT and by students. Such a method allows for discussion of some important things in science writing especially: (a) what constitutes a good opening sentence, (b) the limitations of using AI tools, and (c) tips for improving science writing. This group-discussion approach of LLM application results in the teaching–learning process gives a possibility to underline the AI advances and critically analyze AI application's biases and pitfalls as well as find the most efficient and optimal ways for AI application in the classroom.

No doubt, AI technology will come in different directions in education processes and remain ubiquitous. At the moment, OpenAI's ChatGPT-3.5, Microsoft's Bing, and Google's Bard are free for users. All of these LLM-powered systems give unprecedented writing and analytical power to every teacher and every student. Ethan Mollick from the University of Pennsylvania [11] underlined that experimenting with AI in an ethical, appropriate way can lead to discovering the best approaches and ways to apply pedagogical principles to boost student learning.

Non-profit Contact North/Contact Nord in Ontario, Canada, has released two free AI-powered tools for instructors and students: *AI Teaching Assistant Pro* and *AI Tutor Pro* [40]. Both of these tools are AI-powered and work on smartphones, laptops, and desktops. *AI Teaching Assistant Pro*: (a) creates multiple choice quizzes and essay questions with scoring capability at any level in any subject; (b) creates a syllabus with a course description, learning outcomes, and weekly topics; (c) makes lessons interactive as well as allows teachers more time to help students with critical thinking and conduct discussions. For students, *AI Tutor Pro*, powered by ChatGPT: (a) holds open-ended conversations with students, who can participate by expressing their thoughts and learning about any topic at an academic level; (b) lets students learn at their own pace and individualize their learning experience; (c) includes a review feature to help students remember what they have learned; (d) lets students copy and paste lecture transcripts, notes, and articles into the tutor and discuss the material with it.

The Digital Learning Institute (DLI) uses AI effectively in digital learning and provides a Professional Diploma in Digital Learning Design for students [41]. DLI underlines the five main benefits of AI implementation in digital learning: (1) personalized learning, (2) saving time for instructors and other digital learning professionals, (3) greater insights as machine learning has become an invaluable tool within digital learning, (4) accessibility for neurodivergent learners and students with hearing or visual impairments, as well as for learners staying in different locations, and (5) improved learner experience based on personalized content to learners' needs and rapidly obtaining assessment scores and answers to questions. DLI uses the following ways for AI application in digital learning [41]: knowledge curation, natural language processing, chatbots, and nudges.

The successful cases and the abilities of generative AI for educational purposes are illustrated in [18], including generative AI applications in artwork, coding, writing, research, collaboration, and more. The AI-supported education processes are considered [18] for both (a) formal education in the framework of accredited institutions and (b) non-formal and informal teaching and learning, emphasizing the opportunities for self-learning, group learning, and social change that arise from its implementation.

The perspectives on the multifaceted applications of generative AI in both formal and informal learning environments will grow due to the appearance of new developments in the LLMs. GPT-5, the successor to the already impressive GPT-4, is not just another update; it's a leap toward a future where AI understands and interacts in a more human-like manner [42]. Unlike its predecessors, GPT-5 is expected to excel in multi-modal outputs, meaning it won't just play with text but also images, audio, and possibly video, opening doors to applications we've only dreamed of so far. Sam Altman, CEO of OpenAI, underlined [43] that the main three key GPT-5 breakouts will be:

(1) Multimodality (first of all, "video at the input and output")
(2) Much more advanced reasoning ability (primarily unlocking cognitive abilities)
(3) Reliability (now GPT-4 gives 10K different answers to the same question and doesn't know which one is the best, GPT-5 will give one – the best answer).

2.4 The Role of Academic Consortia in AI Education

One of the perspective approaches to increasing the efficiency of AI specialists' preparation is training students in the framework [44, 45, 46] of academic or academia-AI company consortia. Access to the computing resources that power AI systems is prohibitively expensive and difficult to obtain. These resources [47] are increasingly concentrated in the hands of large technology companies, who maintain outsized control of the AI development ecosystem. As a result, researchers, educational institutions, public interest organizations, and small companies are being left behind, which has enormous implications for AI safety and society.

AI academic consortia will allow for efficiencies of education and research scale not able to be achieved by any single university.

In some cases, cooperation with AI companies can be realized on a bi-agreement basis for solving special tasks. Examples are the cooperation of the Ukrainian Ministry of Digitalization with Google [22], the Albania Government with OpenAI [48], and Arizona State University (ASU) with OpenAI.

ASU collaborates with OpenAI to explore Gen AI potential in education [49]. Through a new partnership, Arizona State University has become the first higher education institution to work with OpenAI to explore the potential of generative AI to enhance teaching and learning. The collaboration brings ChatGPT Enterprise to the university, with the goal "to leverage ASU's intense knowledge core (the faculty, researchers, and staff who drive one of the largest public research universities in the USA) to be at the forefront of discovery and implementation". ASU-OpenAI will take a phased approach to deploying the tool, focusing on its use in three areas: (a) enhancing student success; (b) forging new avenues for innovative research; and (c) streamlining organizational processes.

In most cases, educational consortia as well as AI academic and academic/AI-companies consortia are based on the multi-member style with multi-year activity programs [47, 50–61].

Let us consider several successful cases in creating AI academic and academic/AI-companies consortia.

Case 1. The new "Empire AI" consortium will include seven of New York's leading universities and research institutions [47], including Columbia University, Cornell University, New York University, Rensselaer Polytechnic Institute, the State University of New York (SUNY), the City University of New York (CUNY), and the Simons Foundation, to secure New York's place at the forefront of the artificial intelligence transformation. The Empire AI consortium will create and launch a state-of-the-art AI computing center in Upstate New York to be used by New York's leading institutions to promote responsible research and development, create jobs, etc. Empire AI consortium (a) will create the possibilities for exchanging and sharing resources and accelerate the development of AI centered in the public interest of New York State; (b) will help educational institutions incubate the AI-focused technology startups of the future; (c) will attract high-caliber faculty and expand educational opportunities; and (d) give positive impulse to the creation of responsible AI-based innovations. The consortium will be funded by over US$400 million [42], including US$275 million from the State in grants, and US$125 million from the founding institutions and other private partners such as the Simons Foundation and Tom Secunda.

Case 2. Cambridge's Minderoo Centre for Technology and Democracy is part of a £31 million consortium [50] to create a United Kingdom and international research/innovation ecosystem for responsible and trustworthy AI. The consortium "Responsible AI UK", led by the University of Southampton, will bring together academic and industry partners and will pioneer a reflective, inclusive approach to responsible AI development, working across universities, businesses, the public, and third sectors. The consortium's activities will encompass large-scale research programs, collaborations between academics and businesses, skills programs for the public and industry, and the publication of white papers outlining approaches for the UK and global AI landscape. The

Responsible AI Consortium [51] will serve as a hub for knowledge sharing and resource pooling, allowing individuals and organizations to learn from one another. Activities will include hosting workshops, conferences, and webinars, as well as developing educational resources. It will also facilitate cutting-edge research, the sharing of case studies, and executive education programs in the responsible adoption of generative AI.

Case 3. Auburn University is leading the SEC Artificial Intelligence Consortium to advance innovation in AI teaching and learning [52]. A new Auburn University-designed course "Teaching with AI @ Auburn" will assist the faculty in implementing AI into the classroom. This course has been adopted by the Southeastern Conference (SEC) for use at 14 member institutions of this AI consortium. Auburn University is among several universities delivering pragmatic solutions to critical questions on how faculty can effectively integrate AI into their instruction and scholarship.

Case 4. The Norwegian Artificial Intelligence Research Consortium (NORA) was created for collaboration [53] between eight universities, three university colleges, and five research institutes within AI, machine learning, and robotics. NORA's strategy outlines NORA's vision, mission, ambitions, and strategic goals directed at strengthening Norwegian research, education, and innovation within AI and AI-related fields.

Case 5. The Concord Consortium [54], in collaboration with Texas Tech University, the University of Florida, and WestEd [62], was awarded a US$4 million Education Innovation and Research grant from the US Department of Education. The five-year project will develop a yearlong Artificial Intelligence in Math supplemental certificate program for secondary Algebra 1 or Integrated Math 1 classes.

Case 6. The National Center for Supercomputing Applications [55] was recently announced as a founding member of the Trillion Parameter Consortium, a global gathering of scientists from federal laboratories, research institutes, academia, and industry to address the challenges of building large-scale generative AI systems and advancing trustworthy and reliable AI for scientific discovery. The Trillion Parameter Consortium addresses key challenges in advancing AI for science that include (a) developing scalable model architectures and training strategies, organizing and curating scientific data for training models; (b) optimizing AI libraries for current and future large-scale computing platforms; and (c) developing deep evaluation platforms to assess progress on scientific task learning, reliability, and trust.

Case 7. The Thailand AI University Consortium [63] is a national partnership that unites together Thailand's AI capabilities to drive research and accelerate scientific achievements in AI and high-performance computing. The consortium aims to collaborate, create innovations, and build national AI skills development initiatives delivered through the universities to cultivate the next generation of AI leaders in Thailand.

Case 8. The AI Africa Consortium, led by the University of the Witwatersrand, united Consortium Members with a vested interest in the development of AI research and application in Africa (direction Cirrus) [64]. With the growth in learning, communication, and cooperation with internationally competitive universities there is substantial interest in AI from faculty and students in Africa. The Consortium Members are the universities, research organizations, and government agencies, which are the primary beneficiaries of the infrastructure, engineering capacity, and learning programs.

Case 10. The neuro-symbolic system AlphaGeometry is a neural language model with a symbolic deduction engine [65]. Trained on extensive synthetic data, it serves as a theorem prover for Euclidean plane geometry, generating millions of theorems and proofs without human input. It excels in solving complex problems, successfully tackling 25 out of 30 recent Olympiad-level challenges, surpassing previous methods, and nearing the performance of an average International Mathematical Olympiad gold medalist. Remarkably, AlphaGeometry not only solves all geometry problems under expert evaluation but also generates human-readable proofs.

2.5 Conclusion

The significant role of artificial intelligence tools and systems' applications in increasing the efficiency of research, learning, and teaching processes is discussed in this chapter in detail. Main approaches for AI use in the education field are presented and systematized with a focus on the different groups of users (students, teachers, researchers, and managers), AI roles (tutor, assistant, consultant, and supporter), and AI function descriptions and explanations.

Special attention is paid to the analysis of the interrelations and interconnections between AI and education systems. This is because (a) AI tools and systems can help in qualified cadres' preparation and (b) university graduates in the field of AI can become talented developers of advanced AI at leading companies as OpenAI, Google, Microsoft, DeepMind, and others.

Successful cases and efficient results of AI implementation in education institutions confirm the efficiency of the considered approach. Finally, the consortium approach for AI application in the education sphere based on training students in the framework of the AI academic consortia and academia/AI-company consortia are illustrated by many examples of AI educational consortia from the United States of America, Canada, United Kingdom, Norway, Thailand, and Africa.

Based on this chapter, teachers, researchers, instructional designers, developers, data analysts, programmers, and learners alike can be additionally motivated in AI implementation and find valuable insights into harnessing the power of generative AI for educational purposes.

The next research will be devoted to the development of a set of criteria for the evaluation of the efficiency and quality of graduates' preparation based on their theoretical, design, and practical skills in AI development and implementation for the different fields of human activity.

References

[1] A. Toma, S. Senkaiahliyan, P. R. Lawler, B. Rubin, B. Wang, 'To safely deploy generative AI in health care, models must be open source', Nature, Vol 624, 7 December 2023, pp. 36-38.

[2] Y. Kondratenko, A. Shevchenko, Y. Zhukov, G. Kondratenko, O. Striuk, 'Tendencies and Challenges of Artificial Intelligence Development and Implementation', Proceedings of the 12th IEEE International Conference on Intelligent Data Acquisition and Advanced Computing Systems: Technology and Applications, IDAACS'2023, Vol. 1, 2023, pp. 221 – 226, IDAACS 2023, Dortmund, Germany, 7-9 September 2023.

[3] Y. Kondratenko, A. Shevchenko, Y. Zhukov, V. Slyusar, M. Klymenko, G. Kondratenko, O. Striuk, 'Analysis of the Priorities and Perspectives in Artificial Intelligence Implementation', 13th International IEEE Conference "Dependable Systems, Services and Technologies" (DESSERT'2023), Greece, Athens, October 13-15, 2023.

[4] Y. Kondratenko, G. Kondratenko, A. Shevchenko, V. Slyusar, Y. Zhukov, M. Vakulenko, 'Towards Implementing the Strategy of Artificial Intelligence Development: Ukraine Peculiarities', CEUR Workshop Proceedings, vol. 3513, 2023, pp. 106-117, https://ceur-ws.org/Vol-3513/paper 09.pdf.

[5] P. Lee, C. Golberg, I. Kohane, 'The AI revolution in medicine: GPT-4 and beyond', Pearson Education Inc., 2023.

[6] D. Bulavin, 'What to do so that artificial intelligence does not take away your job, and how it will affect education in Ukraine', July 3, 2023, https://hromadske.ua/posts/sho-robiti-abi-shtuchnij-intelekt-ne-zabrav-u-vas-robotu-i-yak-vin-vpli ne-na-osvitu-v-ukrayini

[7]   T. Biloborodova, I. Skarga-Bandurova, 'Human-AI Collaboration in Decision Making: An Initial Reliability Study and Methodology', 2023 IEEE 12th International Conference on Intelligent Data Acquisition and Advanced Computing Systems: Technology and Applications (IDAACS), Dortmund, Germany, 2023, pp. 1151-1155, doi:10.1109/IDAACS58523.2023.10348 928.

[8]   D. Leitão, P. Saleiro, M. A. T. Figueiredo, P. Bizarro, 'Human-AI Collaboration in Decision-Making: Beyond Learning to Defer', arXiv:2206.13202, https://arxiv.org/abs/2206.13202

[9]   Y. P. Kondratenko, N. Y. Kondratenko, 'Reduced library of the soft computing analytic models for arithmetic operations with asymmetrical fuzzy numbers', in: Soft Computing: Developments, Methods and Applications, A. Casey (Ed), NOVA Science Publishers, Hauppauge, New York, 2016, pp. 1-38.

[10]   Y. Kondratenko, N. Kondratenko, 'Real-Time Fuzzy Data Processing Based on a Computational Library of Analytic Models', Data, Volume 3, Issue 4, 59, pp.1-19, 2018, doi:10.3390/data3040059.

[11]   O. Kozlov, G. Kondratenko, Z. Gomolka, Y. Kondratenko, 'Synthesis and Optimization of Green Fuzzy Controllers for the Reactors of the Specialized Pyrolysis Plants', in: V. Kharchenko, et al. (eds), Green IT Engineering: Social, Business and Industrial Applications, Studies in Systems, Decision and Control, vol. 171, Springer, Cham, pp. 373-396, 2019, DOI: https://doi.org/10.1007/978-3-030-00253-4_16

[12]   Z. Gomolka, E. Dudek-Dyduch, Y. Kondratenko, 'From homogeneous network to neural nets with fractional derivative mechanism', International Conference on Artificial Intelligence and Soft Computing, ICAISC-2017, Rutkowski, L. et al. (Eds), Part I, Zakopane, Poland, 11-15 June 2017, LNAI 10245, Springer, Cham, pp. 52-63, 2017. DOI https://doi.org/10.1007/978-3-319-59063-9_5

[13]   M. Gault, 'Eric Schmidt Thinks AI Is as Powerful as Nukes', 2022, https://bit.ly/3f1T3ie.

[14]   'From Einstein to AI: how 100 years have shaped science', Editorials, Nature, Vol. 624, 21/28 December 2023, p. 474.

[15]   M. Ghassemi, A. Birhane, M. Bilal, S. Kankaria, C. Malone, E. Mollick, F. Tustumi, 'ChatGPT one year on who is using it, how and why?', Nature, Vol. 624, pp. 39-41, 7 December 2023.

[16]   M. Hutson, 'Will Superintelligentai Sneak Up on Us? Study Suggests Not', Nature, Vol. 625, p. 223, 11 January 2024.

[17]   D. Castelvecchi, 'DeepMind AI Outdoes Human Mathematicians on Unsolved Problem', Nature, Vol 625, pp. 12-13, 4 January 2024.

[18] S. Hai-Jew, 'Generative AI in teaching and learning', 5 December 2023, DOI10.4018/979-8-3693-0074-9, https://www.scopus.com/record/display.uri?eid=2-s2.0-8518 2286246&origin=recordpage

[19] L. Wesemann, 'The promise and perils of AI in academia', University of Melbourne, Australia, https://www.youtube.com/watch?v=i8lmyaB7sH4

[20] 'ChatGPT caught NYC schools off guard. Now, we're determined to embrace its potential', 2023, https://ny.chalkbeat.org/2023/5/18/23727942/chatgp t-nyc-schools-david-banks

[21] 'Seoul Education Office to Introduce Robots for 1:1 English Learning', KBS, 29 November 2023, world.kbs.co.kr/service/news_view.htm?lang=e&Seq_Code=18 2095

[22] M. Klymkovetskyi, 'The Ministry of Digitization and Google are launching a free course on artificial intelligence for Ukrainians', 3 May 2023, https://hromadske.ua/posts/mincifri-i-google-zapuskayut-dlya-ukrayinciv-bezplatnij-kur s-pro-shtuchnij-intelekt

[23] D. Bulavin, 'The Ministry of Education and Science has launched a test based on artificial intelligence, which can help students determine their future profession', July 29, 2023, https://hromadske.ua/posts/mon-zapustilo-test-na-o snovi-shtuchnogo-intelektu-yakij-mozhe-dopomogti-uchnyam-viznachiti-majbutnyu-profesiyu

[24] A. Joshi, M. Vinay, P. Bhaskar, 'Impact of coronavirus pandemic on the Indian education sector: perspectives of teachers on online teaching and assessments', Interactive Technology and Smart Education, Volume 18, Issue 2, pp. 205-226, 2021, DOI10.1108/ITSE-06-2020-0087

[25] A. I. Shevchenko, M. S. Klymenko, 'Developing a Model of Artificial Conscience', 15th IEEE International Scientific and Technical Conference on Computer Sciences and Information Technologies, CSIT'2020, Vol. 1, 23-26 September 2020, Lviv-Zbarazh, pp. 51–54, 2020.

[26] 'Top 7 Ways Artificial Intelligence Is Used in Education', 2021, https://bit.ly /3DyW5Vp.

[27] D. Castelvecchi, 'How will AI change mathematics?', Nature, vol. 615, pp. 15-16, 2 March 2023,.

[28] O. Striuk, Y. Kondratenko, 'Generative Adversarial Neural Networks and Deep Learning: Successful Cases and Advanced Approaches', International Journal of Computing, Vol. 20, Issue 3, pp. 339-349, 2021.

[29] R. Duro and Y. Kondratenko (Eds)., 'Advances in Intelligent Robotics and Collaborative Automation', River Publishers, Aalborg, 2015.

[30] V. M. Kuntsevich, V. F. Gubarev, Y. P. Kondratenko, D. V. Lebedev, and V. P. Lysenko (Eds)., 'Control Systems: Theory and Applications', River Publishers, Girsrup, Delft, 2018.

[31] I. Atamanyuk et al., 'Computational method of the cardiovascular diseases classification based on a generalized nonlinear canonical

decomposition of random sequences', Scientific Reports, Vol. 13, 59, 2023, https://doi.org/10.1038/s41598-022-27318-0

[32] M. Tetyana, Y. Kondratenko, I. Sidenko, G. Kondratenko, 'Computer Vision Mobile System for Education Using Augmented Reality Technology', Journal of Mobile Multimedia, vol. 17, no. 4, pp. 555-576, 2021.

[33] Y. Kondratenko, I. Atamanyuk, I. Sidenko, G. Kondratenko, S. Sichevskyi, 'Machine Learning Techniques for Increasing Efficiency of the Robot's Sensor and Control Information Processing', Sensors, vol. 22, no. 3, 1062, Jan. 2022, https://doi.org/10.3390/s22031062

[34] A.N., Tkachenko, et al., 'Evolutionary adaptation of control processes in robots operating in non-stationary environments', Mechanism and Machine Theory, Vol. 18, No. 4, Print. Great Britain, pp. 275-278, 1983, DOI:10.1016/0094-114X(83)90118-0

[35] C. Basgier, S. Sharma, 'Should scientists delegate their writing to ChatGPT?', Nature, Vol 624, p. 523, 21/28 December 2023.

[36] S. Canali, F. Barone-Adesi, 'Can AI deliver advice that misjudgment-free for science policy?', Nature, Vol. 624, p. 252, 14 December 2023.

[37] R. Sharma, 'How Gemini Nano is Redefining Mobile Capabilities', 23 January, 2024, https://markovate.com/blog/gemini-nano/.

[38] 'StableLM Zephyr 3B GGUF', 27 January, 2024, https://huggingface.co/brittlewis12/stablelm-zephyr-3b-GGUF.

[39] S. Chauhan, 'Rabbit Unveils Innovative Virtual Assistant R1 at CES 2024', 10 January 2024, https://bnnbreaking.com/tech/rabbit-unveils-innovative-virtual-assistant-r1-at-ces-2024/.

[40] 'Free AI Teaching Assistant and AI Tutor Powered by ChatGPT', Campus Technology, 30 November 2023. https://campustechnology.com/articles/2023/11/30/free-ai-teaching-assistant-and-ai-tutor-powered-by-chatgpt.aspx?admgarea=News

[41] 'AI in Digital Learning: Benefits, Applications and Challenges', Digital Learning Institute, 29 September 2023.

[42] V. Paradkar, 'The Next Leap in AI: OpenAI's Journey Towards GPT-5', 12 January 2024, https://medium.com/@virajsparadkar/the-next-leap-in-ai-openais-journey-towards-gpt-5-844f0a8d1d2d

[43] 'GPT-5 Is Coming In 2024? Sam Altman Announces Updates at Y Combinator W24', https://www.youtube.com/watch?v=qfPyVuxf4o0

[44] G. Kondratenko, et al., 'Fuzzy Decision Making System for Model-Oriented Academia/Industry Cooperation: University Preferences', in: Berger-Vachon, C., et al. (eds.), Complex Systems: Solutions and Challenges in Economics, Management and Engineering, Studies in Systems, Decision and Control, vol. 125, Springer, Berlin, Heidelberg, pp. 109-124, 2018.

[45] Y. Kondratenko, et al., 'University Curricula Modification Based on Advancements in Information and Communication Technologies', CEUR Workshop Proceedings, 1614, pp.184–199, 2016.

[46] Y.P. Kondratenko, et al., 'Knowledge-Based Decision Support System with Reconfiguration of Fuzzy Rule Base for Model-Oriented Academic-Industry Interaction', in: Gil-Lafuente, A.M., et al. (eds.), Applied Mathematics and Computational Intelligence, FIM 2015, Advances in Intelligent Systems and Computing, vol. 730, Springer, Cham, pp. 101-112, 2018.

[47] 'Governor Hochul Unveils Fifth Proposal of 2024 State of the State: Empire AI Consortium to Make New York the National Leader in AI Research and Innovation', January 8, 2024, Albany, NY, https://www.gove rnor.ny.gov/news/governor-hochul-unveils-fifth-proposal-2024-state-state-empire-ai-consortiu m-make-new-york

[48] A. Taylor, 'Albania to speed up EU accession using ChatGPT', EURACTIV, 12 December 2023, https://www.euractiv.com/section/politics/news /albania-to-speed-up-eu-accession-using-chatgpt/

[49] 'Arizona State University Partners with OpenAI to Explore Gen AI Potential in Education', Campus Technology, 18 January 2024, https://ca mpustechnology.com/Articles/2024/01/18/Arizona-State-University-Partners-with-OpenAI-to-Explore-Gen-AI-Potential-in-Education.aspx

[50] 'Cambridge academics join £31 million consortium to develop trustworthy and secure AI', Cambridge University, 14 June 2023, https://www.cam.ac.uk/research/news/cambridge-academics-join-ps31-million-consortium-to-develop-trustworthy-and-secure-ai

[51] 'Responsible AI Institute Launches Inaugural Consortium; Operationalizes AI Safety Across Industries', InsideBIGDATA, 1 July 2023, https://insidebigdata.com/2023/07/01/responsible-ai-institute-launches-inaugural-con sortium-operationalizes-ai-safety-across-industries/

[52] 'Auburn University leading SEC consortium to advance innovation in AI teaching, learning', Auburn University, 7 August 2023, https://ocm.auburn.edu /newsroom/news_articles/2023/08/071326-auburn-leading-sec-ai-teaching-consortium.php

[53] 'Norwegian Artificial Intelligence Research Consortium, NORA. https://ww w.nora.ai/

[54] 'New AI in Math program is funded by the U.S. Department of Education', Concord Consortium, January 4, 2024, https://concord.org/blog /tag/artificial-intelligence/

[55] A. Helregel, 'NCSA Helps Found Trillion Parameter Consortium', NCSA, 27 November 2023. https://www.ncsa.illinois.edu/ncsa-helps-found-trillion-parameter-co nsortium/

[56] O. Shurbin, et al., 'Computerized system for cooperation model's selection based on intelligent fuzzy technique', CEUR Workshop Proceedings 2516, pp. 206-217, 2019.

[57] M. Solesvik, et al., 'Architecture for Collaborative Digital Simulation for the Polar Regions', in: V. Kharchenko, et al. (eds), Green IT Engineering: Social, Business and Industrial Applications, Studies in Systems, Decision and Control, vol 171, Springer, Cham, pp. 517-531, 2019, DOI:https://doi.org/10.1007/978-3-030-00253-4_22

[58] V. Shebanin, et al., 'Development of the Mathematical Model of the Informational Resource of a Distance Learning System', in: O. Chertov, et al. (eds.), Recent Developments in Data Science and Intelligent Analysis of Information, Proceedings of the XVIII International Conference on Data Science and Intelligent Analysis of Information, June 4–7, 2018, Kyiv, Ukraine. ICDSIAI 2018, Advances in Intelligent Systems and Computing, Vol. 836, Springer International Publishing, pp. 199-205, 2019, DOI:10.1007/978-3-319-97885-7_20

[59] Y. Kondratenko, G. Kondratenko, I. Sidenko, 'Intelligent Decision Support System for Selecting the University-Industry Cooperation Model Using Modified Antecedent-Consequent Method', in: J. Medina et al. (eds), Information Processing and Management of Uncertainty in Knowledge-Based Systems: Theory and Foundations, 17th International Conference, IPMU 2018, Cadiz, Spain, June 11–15, 2018, Proceedings, Part II, CCIS 854, Springer International Publishing AG, pp. 596–607, 2018, https://doi.org/10.1007/978-3-319-91476-3_49

[60] M. Solesvik, et al., 'Joint Digital Simulation Platforms for Safety and Preparedness', in: Luo Y. (eds), Cooperative Design, Visualization, and Engineering, CDVE 2018, Lecture Notes in Computer Science, vol. 11151, Springer, Cham, pp. 118-125, 2018, DOI:https://doi.org/10.1007/978-3-030-00560-3_16

[61] V. Shebanin, et al., 'Application of Fuzzy Predicates and Quantifiers by Matrix Presentation in Informational Resources Modeling', Perspective Technologies and Methods in MEMS Design: Proceedings of the International Conference MEMSTECH-2016. Lviv-Poljana, Ukraine, April 20-24, pp. 146-149, 2016, DOI:10.1109/MEMSTECH.2016.7507536

[62] WestEd, https://www.wested.org/

[63] 'An MOU signing ceremony was held by Thailand A.I. University Consortium', Thailand A.I. University Consortium, 3 December 2020, https://th-ai.org/

[64] 'AI Africa Consortium', https://aiafrica.ac.za/

[65] T. H. Trinh, et al., 'Solving olympiad geometry without human demonstrations', Nature, vol. 625, pp. 476–482, 2024, https://doi.org/10.1038/s41586-023-06747-5.

Authors' Short CV

Yuriy Kondratenko is a Doctor of Science, Professor, Honour Inventor of Ukraine (2008), Corr. Academician of Royal Academy of Doctors (Barcelona, Spain), Head of the Department of Intelligent Information Systems at Petro Mohyla Black Sea National University (PMBSNU), Ukraine, Leading Researcher of the Institute of Artificial Intelligence Problems of MES and NAS of Ukraine. He has received (a) a Ph.D. (1983) and Dr.Sc. (1994) in Elements and Devices of Computer and Control Systems from Odessa National Polytechnic University, (b) several international grants and scholarships for conducting research at Institute of Automation of Chongqing University, P.R. China (1988–1989), Ruhr-University Bochum, Germany (2000, 2010), Nazareth College and Cleveland State University, USA (2003), (c) Fulbright Scholarship for researching in USA (2015/2016) at the Dept. of Electrical Engineering and Computer Science in Cleveland State University. Research interests include robotics, automation, sensors and control systems, intelligent decision support systems, and fuzzy logic.

Vadym Slyusar is a Doctor of Science, Professor, Honoured Scientist and Technician of Ukraine (2008). He received a Ph.D. in 1992, Doctor of Sciences in 2000, and Professor in 2005. His research interests include radar systems, smart antennas for wireless communications and digital beamforming, artificial intelligence, and robotics.

Maryna Solesvik is a professor of Innovation and Management at Western Norway University of Applied Sciences. Earlier she served as a professor and chair of Maritime Innovation at Nord University. She holds Ph.D. degrees from the Nord University Business School (Norway) and the Institute of Agrarian Economics (Ukraine). She served as a board member of several Norwegian companies and organizations, including Riksteatret.

Her research interests are entrepreneurial intentions, female entrepreneurship, entrepreneurship in emerging economies, maritime business, and technology innovation.

Nina Kondratenko is a Ph.D. student at Darla Moore School of Business, University of South Carolina, USA. Mrs. Kondratenko is a Fulbright scholar from Ukraine. She holds an M.A. with honors from Taras Shevchenko Kyiv National University, Ukraine, as well as an M.A. from the University of South Carolina, USA. Her methodology is focused on the application of fuzzy logic and other artificial intelligence techniques. Research interests range from sustainability-supporting policies to corporate social responsibility practices in emerging markets. She has published the research results as articles (in international journals Data and Journal of International Business Studies), book chapters (in Studies in Fuzziness and Soft Computing, Advances in Intelligent Systems and Computing, Soft Computing: Developments, Methods and Applications, Decision-Making: Processes, Behavioral Influences and Role in Business Management) and conference papers (CEUR Workshop Proceedings, Proceedings of the 2018 IEEE 2nd International Conference on Data Stream Mining and Processing, DSMP 2018).

Zbigniew Gomolka is Assistant Professor, Head of the Computer Sciences and Image Processing Laboratory at the Centre for Innovation and Transfer of Technical and Natural Knowledge, Institute of Computer Science, University of Rzeszow, Poland. He is a specialist in artificial intelligence, especially in the fields of neural network training algorithms, eye-tracking technologies in HMI systems, and optimization of logistic tasks for UAV systems in the conditions of dynamically changing system resources. Active Erasmus + program member.

3

Multivariate Information Systems and Polymetric Sensors: AI Implementation Perspective in Shipping and Shipbuilding

Yu. D. Zhukov [1,2] **and O. V. Zivenko** [2]

[1] "C-Job Nikolayev" LLC, Mykolaiv, Ukraine
[2] Marine Instrumentation Department, Admiral Makarov National University of Shipbuilding, Mykolaiv, Ukraine
E-mail: y.zhukov@c-job.com.ua, oleksii.zivenko@nuos.edu.ua

Abstract

The relevance of this chapter lies in the increasingly global impact of AI's methods and instruments on accelerating the dual transition of the maritime industry, including shipping, shipbuilding, and critical maritime infrastructure. The purpose of the research is a concise and structured review of some gaps in the development and implementation of the concepts of e-navigation, Digital Twins, IIOT, etc., and their potential influence on the safety and overall efficiency of commercial ships and onshore transshipment terminals. In the process of writing this chapter, several innovative and patented technical solutions in a general subject area were analyzed and systemized. Using the method of heuristic design from the perspective of a timely and effective dual transition of the maritime industry, modified added value chains and separate concepts and solutions were identified and proposed. Analogies were also used to develop practical structures of appropriate monitoring and control systems since using AI instruments to optimize dual transition task solutions is relatively efficiently solved in other industries, namely in communication, automotive, robotics, healthcare industries, etc. The concept of "multivariate control of a multifunctional ship fleet" based on the advantages of polymetric sensors utilization and edge and cloud computing hybridization is described concisely, somewhat limited by the number of case studies conducted, but in a meaningful and structured way as a result of the research.

Keywords: Dual transition, multifunctional ships' fleet, multivariate measurement, supply chain optimization, ship safety, hybrid computing, data analytics, connectivity.

3.1 Introduction

At the beginning of this millennium, the global challenges to mankind became more acute, primarily related to man-made climate change, the exhaustion of natural energy and food resources, and the overpopulation of the planet [1, 2]. The scientific and technical community was among the first to participate in analyzing the situation and developing appropriate mechanisms to overcome these problems [3–5].

High-growth technology industries include clean energy, AI, next-generation communications and advanced manufacturing, as mentioned in [6, 7]. To date, the relevant international legislation and investment policies of most leading countries and their associations have changed significantly and focus primarily on dual (green and digital) transition, including industrial transformation based on the paradigm of Industry 5.0 [8–10].

Such industries as ICT (including IST and AI), robotics and automotive, space and aircraft, and metrology are still leading at the digitalization level [11–14] and have recently paid increasing attention to green transition, where the energy sector is leading [15]. Ongoing research in the rapidly evolving field of CPS modeling addresses challenges such as scalability, interoperability, connectivity, and integration of emerging technologies.

Similar processes are taking place in the shipping and shipbuilding industries but at a much slower pace. Still, diverse autonomous and electric vessels and robots, ICT, and mobile applications are reshaping the maritime economy and rapidly becoming mainstream, user-friendly practices in ships' navigation and manufacturing. For those who can innovate fast, there is a once-in-a-century opportunity now to leapfrog the competition, leverage existing capabilities, and win the race to lead in the new mobility era.

The global artificial intelligence (AI) market was valued at approximately US$87 billion in 2022 and is expected to reach US$407 billion by the end of 2027, growing at a CAGR of around 36.2% between 2022 and 2027 [16]. The global shipbuilding market is projected to grow at a CAGR of 7.4% in the 2023–2030 period, starting from US$355.1 billion in 2022 and reaching US$892.7 billion by the end of 2030 [17].

The primary factors responsible for both markets' growth are the emergence of various green fuel implementations, AI-based business models, and the growth of the already highly competitive costs of waterborne cargo shipping. AI has been set up as the primary driver of growing technologies, such as robotics, big data, and IoT. In both the short-term and the long-term, and across back- and front-office applications, AI can add value to business workflows, augment employee capabilities and harness the power of man and machine to improve customer experience.

This research drafts a roadmap for implementing AI instruments in the maritime domain, focusing on the novel ships and ships' fleet concepts designated to solve dual transition challenges via integrating some innovative solutions from both industries.

3.2 Role of Metrology in AI Implementation in Maritime Industries

The role of metrology and sensors in maritime industries' supply chains, including smart ships, smart shipyards, navigation, transshipment, and process control, is acknowledged [18, 19]. Metrology plays a similar role in the development and success of industrial intelligence systems, as smart sensors are the "eyes, ears, and tactile sensors" of AI systems.

Metrology refers to the science of measurement and, in the context of AI, it involves ensuring the accuracy, precision, and reliability of the data collected by sensors. Sensors provide AI systems with the necessary input to interact with the physical world. Accurate and reliable sensor data is essential for AI systems to make informed decisions, learn from their environment, and develop new solutions. Metrology plays a significant role in calibrating and validating these sensors, ensuring that the data they collect is trustworthy and can be used effectively by AI algorithms. By combining metrology and sensor technology, AI systems can develop and implement new promising solutions across various industries and applications.

The remarkable convergence of digitalization and manufacturing is evidently reshaping industrial landscapes, including shipbuilding and other services in maritime infrastructure sectors, in an era known as Industry 5.0 [19]. Nevertheless, current technologies used on ships and onshore stations to avoid wrecks, collisions, and contact between ships are not enough to prevent the number of maritime accidents with high yearly economic costs, significant environmental impact, and, unfortunately, the loss of lives [20].

Before the marine industry, there are other inevitable challenges – the need for an accelerated decrease in harmful emissions in the environment, the transition to clean green fuels and renewable energy sources, a sharp decrease in OPEX, CAPEX of seagoing ships and fleets with minimization of downtime and long transitions in ballast (without useful cargo), purification of ocean and sea waters from plastic and synthetic garbage and many others. Such a situation stimulates intensive innovations, providing a competitive basis for comparing and promoting AI integration, ICT, and CPS optimization capabilities for joint supply chains of all sectors and stakeholders of the marine industry.

3.3 Prospects of AI Implementation in Maritime Industries

In today's rapidly evolving business landscape of the maritime industry, the convergence of sustainable supply chain management (SSCM) and machine intelligence, encompassing artificial intelligence and machine learning (ML), represents an extremely dynamic and transformative nexus [21].

The digitalization and connectivity of all its appropriate links in the shipbuilding supply chain are recognized as critical for companies operating in engineering-to-order industries striving to increase the competitiveness and profitability of their fleets [22]. Over the years, several innovative methods have optimized supply chains and decision-making in uncertain conditions. An innovative method of prioritizing supply chain optimization strategies based on associated general cost, overall effectiveness, and manageability of appropriate supply processes was proposed in [23]. A simulation study was used within a theoretically grounded framework of Bayesian belief networks. A framework for selecting sustainable suppliers using an integrated compensatory fuzzy AHP-TOPSIS multi-criteria approach was proposed in [24] and further developed in [25]. An intelligent decision support scheme for ship navigation in narrow channels in uncertain conditions and a method based on optical color-logic gates were presented in [26, 27].

3.3.1 The Ocean's Plastic Pollution Challenge

One of humanity's most demanding challenges remains the long-lasting and drastically progressing pollution of rivers and the world's oceans by plastic debris [28, 29]. More than five trillion plastic particles are floating in the ocean's five largest convergence zones, and about 300 million tons of plastic are produced yearly, accelerating ocean pollution [30, 31]. It was recognized as one of the most urgent problems and a natural rock on the way to a cleaner future for the planet [32].

The fight against water pollution has a long and successful history, and some significant results have been achieved with active financial support through grants and international funds. However, according to the classification of plastic debris cleaning tasks and their KPI assessment [33], it is evident that not all are solved at an equal pace. A summary of definitions for classifying each solution consists of four functions (prevention, monitoring, cleaning and multiuse of the three previous), litter size (macro, micro and nano) and the set of application areas, namely inland waters (rivers, lakes, canals, WWT), coastline (ports, coastal waters, outlet/inlets, fjords, estuaries, and beaches), seas, open oceans, and vertical domain (water surface, including subsurface, water column, and sea/river bottom).

In spite of intensive attention from society, governments, and philanthropists to the above challenges, relatively few litter-cleaning systems have been developed and used [33]. The experts from different domains have rather skeptical forecasts concerning the time, cost, and efficiency of existing practical solutions to the problem without nontrivial ones proposed by naval architects and mechanical engineers [34–37].

That is why many companies started making products from recycled materials to bring their environmentally friendly practices based on the latest patent to the forefront [38, 39]. For example, several technical solutions for recycling solid plastic waste on ships into recycled plastic granules [40, 41], into liquid hydrocarbon fuel [42–45] or into hydrogen as fuel [46] were patented and implemented.

Naval architects joined in solving the problem of collecting plastic garbage from the oceans' waters. Recently, many new patented solutions have appeared to create vessels that collect plastic waste. For example, vessels that collect waste on the water surface [42–47], lost synthetic fishing nets [48], and plastic debris at some depth under the water surface [49], etc.

3.3.2 Further Development of the OPUSS Project

The idea of the OPUSS Project (Ocean Plastics Utilization Ship System) [37] was to develop a fleet of ships and floating structures for the processing of plastics at sites of litter localization. Such a fleet will clean up the ocean of plastic waste with optimal results regarding integrated logistical efficiency, optimization of the nomenclature of fleet vessels and their projects, and the minimal operating costs of the overall recycling process.

The next step in the development of the OPUSS system is to bring all production facilities and equipment to the requirements of dual transition by minimizing air emissions, maximum use of autonomous vessels and floating installations with clean power plants or hybrid power units based on solar panels, wind turbines, hydrogen batteries, green fuels such as ammonia, natural gas, hydrogen, etc. Obviously, such modernization is impossible without the complex application of modern smart sensors, digitalization, and automation of most processes using artificial intelligence tools.

The fleet of vessels of various types proposed in the article [37] is intended for the disposal of plastic garbage polluting the waters of the oceans, consists of several vessels equipped with specialized equipment for collecting plastic garbage and at least one central floating module equipped with specialized equipment for the processing of plastic garbage to the products ready for reuse.

The general structure of the multifunctional ocean cleaning fleet (OCF) is based on the initial OPUSS concept and is shown in Figure 3.1 [50, 51]. It refers to a fleet of vehicles and assets that can perform multiple tasks or functions. Instead of having separate fleets for different purposes, such as ocean plastic garbage fishing, sorting and transportation, delivery to places of plastic recycling plants, maintenance of ships, or other services, a multifunctional fleet combines all these functions into a single fleet.

In Figure 3.1, the following designations are taken: 1 – multifunctional ocean cleaning fleet; 2 – ocean plastic recycling ship; 3 – recycled plastic transocean shuttles; 4 – plastic local transport shuttles; 5 – ocean plastic garbage patches; 6 – ocean garbage fishing ships; 7 – garbage storage and sorting facilities; 8 – garbage to granules recycling plant; 9 – garbage to diesel recycling plant.

The general management of the OCF can optimize its resources and increase operational efficiency by installing an MVC on its ships and implementing most of the available ICT and AI instruments in the near future. But even changing the initial ocean cleanup logistic scheme [36, 37] only (Figure 3.2) to one of the proposed concepts of a multifunctional ocean cleanup fleet provides

Figure 3.1: The general structure of the multifunctional ocean cleaning fleet concept.

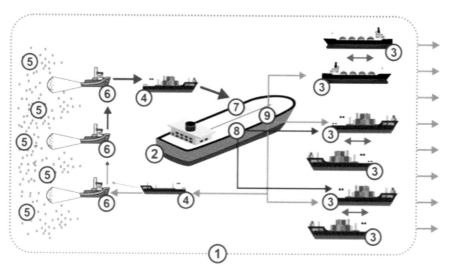

Figure 3.2: Initial ocean cleanup logistic scheme.

a tangible, positive outcome by radically changing the reverse logistic model to the localized circular scenario to ensure the reduced time of ocean cleanup refinancing, optimized operational cost, and reduced ecological risks.

According to the concept of the OCF, being a multifunctional ships fleet (MSF) includes a set of required vehicles and production shops that are versatile and equipped with the necessary tools, sensors, and equipment to perform different prescribed functions that meet mobile connectivity requirements [20, 56].

The vehicles' specialized features and designs allow them to operate under a joint final objective – effectively collecting and recycling plastic and synthetic litter from ocean waters into products ready for reuse. The concept of the ocean plastic and synthetic litter recycling ship is presented in Figure 3.3 [52].

Figure 3.3: Ocean plastic and synthetic litter recycling ship concept scheme.

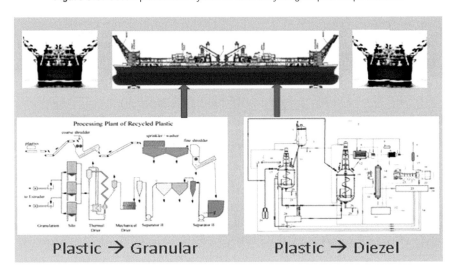

Additionally, OCF operating teams must have precisely measured information prerequisites for proper scheduling and coordination of fleet processes to ensure adaptive and optimal utilization of all participating ships in a timely and efficient manner.

To provide these features, the concept of multivariate control (MVC) of the multifunctional ship fleet (MSF) based on the advantages of smart sensors and hybrid (edge plus cloud) computing is proposed for detailed development, introduction, engineering, testing, and implementation.

The logistic scheme presented in Figure 3.4 provides tangible commercial (cost reduction), ecological (no transfer of exotic flora to other regions), and time-saving effects (nearly ten times shorter ROI period) that support the overall feasibility of the ocean cleaning mission in a generally observed period of time [37].

Another example of the potential use of the MVC concept is the fleet of autonomous unmanned underwater dredgers (AUMD) [53–55] (Figure 3.5) in combination with uncrewed surface vessels (USV), designed for autonomous

Figure 3.4: Alternative ocean cleanup logistic scheme.

inspection, logistic and surveillance operations, including mapping the current depth and three-dimensional topography of bottoms of seas and lakes, rivers, and canals [56].

The abovementioned AI instruments should be effectively implemented based on the multifunctional ship fleet paradigm in both cases. Later, it can be done in similar cases. However, it will succeed only when followed by the application of comprehensive sets of different smart sensors. New and more intelligent tools are needed to anticipate the dynamic shipping events at open seas and other water areas.

Figure 3.5: General view and cross-section of an AUMD.

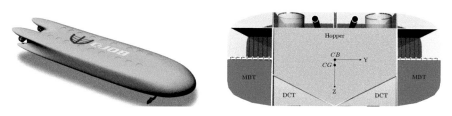

These new tools should be smart enough to identify dangerous and operational situations before they happen. Ships with this technology were called "smart ships" in [20]. Simply put, we are talking about the prospects of transition to the options of using a "smart fleet of smart ships" (SFSS) to solve the considered and similar problems of dual transition of the maritime industry.

The efficiency of the recycled plastic transocean shuttles requires separate consideration, which, unlike the plastic local transport shuttles, delivers cargo in the form of recycled and ready-for-reuse plastic and synthetic debris to various remote ports from the location of the fleet. In other words, they communicate operationally with the "outside world." This requires appropriate coordination with port authorities, including oil terminal operators. However, it should be noted that the maritime infrastructure sector also has some features related to the secrecy of commercial information.

Most transshipment terminals are equipped with modern systems of accounting and control of the flow of oil products and gases in their tanks [62–66]. This allows them, both retrospectively and prospectively, to keep track of their ability to receive goods on a flexible schedule, which is essential for the OCF fleet. The systems described in the [64–66] work according to a common standard on both shore and ship systems using information coding, making them prospective for use in the multivariate control of multifunctional ships fleet paradigm. In addition, these polymeric systems differ in that they use a single transducer to measure several parameters of liquid media and gases (level, section of unbreakable media, temperature, composition, and pressure of gas mixtures). This structure fully meets the requirements of digital and green transformation.

3.3.3 Metrological Aspects of Multivariate Control Concept Development

Metrological aspects of MVC concept development require the considerations and techniques used to measure and analyze multiple variables to develop effective control of multiple ships of various types as members of one of SFSS, in our example, OCF or AUMD+USV. In this context, metrology is responsible for measuring and assessing the quality and accuracy of the data collected from embedded sensors and onboard instruments to provide successful solutions to the MVC system.

The dual transition to smart sensors and other instruments in the maritime industry requires specific requirements to be met. Firstly, there is a need for advanced technology and infrastructure to support the integration of smart sensors and instruments. This includes reliable, high-speed communication networks, data storage and processing capabilities, and compatible hardware and software systems.

Secondly, all sensors must have standardized protocols and interfaces to ensure seamless communication and interoperability between different sensors and instruments. This would allow robust exchange of data and information in a unified and efficient manner. Additionally, the SFSS and each ship's personnel must be trained to operate and maintain these smart sensors and instruments effectively. Training and education programs should be in place in advance to equip maritime professionals with the necessary knowledge and skills to utilize these technologies. This task is a real challenge to college and universitiy faculties, one of the most conservative industries along with shipbuilding. Also, all subsystems must ensure the safe and responsible use of smart sensors and instruments in the maritime industry, safely addressing data privacy issues, cybersecurity, and compliance with international standards and regulations. Only by meeting these requirements can the dual transition to smart sensors and other smart instruments, as described in [60–66], be successfully implemented in the maritime industry, improving safety, efficiency, and sustainability.

3.3.4 Discussion of AI-based Multivariate Control Concept Prospects

Ensuring that the measurements are reliable and consistent is crucial to accurately and timely represent any MSF activities and all functional processed data. Multivariate control concept development involves analyzing measured data, relationships, and interactions between different variables to identify patterns, correlations, and dependencies. This allows resilient development of control strategies that consider the complex dynamics and interdependencies of the system, leading to more efficient and effective control actions.

Accordingly, specialized ML models should be designed and used to improve, for example, OCF performance efficiency by exposing them to more data concerning litter-catching and recycling processes from ships' sensory monitoring systems [63, 64]. The iterative learning process of the OCF ML application enables it to continuously refine its predictions and recommendations on fleets' logistics and overall supply chain management [65–66]. For instance, transportation forecasting models can adapt to changing ships' behavior, while logistics optimization algorithms can adjust to cargo handling and delivery fluctuations.

It is a logical next step to engage AIS technology to provide overall informational connectivity of individual ships via onboard MVC systems. It allows the provision of sharing the data from mobile applications, similar to MobileAIS and SmartAIS [20], to the private cloud of MVC and to other ships' embedded control systems and improves the quality of predictions and operations optimization proposals using big data analytics, cognitive and predictive maintenance tools, etc.

Ongoing research in the rapidly evolving field of AI methods and instrument applications based on cyber-physical systems modeling concerning specifics of maritime innovative sensor complexes addresses challenges such as scalability, interoperability, and integrating emerging disruptive technologies.

The future of edge, cloud, and hybrid platforms will combine increased connectivity, improved data processing capabilities, and enhanced collaboration between devices and hybrid systems, including blockchain technology. Edge computing, which involves processing data closer to the source rather than sending it to the cloud, is anticipated to become more prevalent as the number of connected devices grows. This will enable faster response times, reduced network traffic, and improved reliability for real-time data analysis applications. On the other hand, cloud computing will continue to play a crucial role in storing and processing large volumes of data, providing scalability and flexibility to businesses.

Hybrid platforms, which integrate both edge and cloud computing, may become more common in maritime industry applications as its stakeholders and managers seek to optimize their infrastructure and take advantage of the benefits offered by both approaches. The proposed hybrid model of the multivariate control concept will allow for efficient data processing and storage, ensuring the best resource utilization while meeting different application requirements. Overall, the future of edge, cloud, and hybrid platforms holds excellent potential for enabling advanced technologies such as artificial intelligence, the Internet of Things, and autonomous systems, fostering innovation and driving digital transformation across industries.

3.4 Conclusions

Some gaps were analyzed in implementing AI concepts, methods, and instruments in maritime industries based on examples of current dual transition challenges and their potential influence on the safety and overall efficiency of commercial ships and onshore transshipment terminals. In the process of writing this paper, a number of innovative and patented technical solutions in a general subject area were analyzed and systemized. Using the method of heuristic design from the perspective of a timely and effective dual transition of the maritime industry, modified added value chains and separate concepts and solutions were identified and proposed.

The research also delved into the implications of these concepts on business models, workforce dynamics, and the overall future landscape of shipping and shipbuilding. It is a valuable resource for professionals and researchers seeking to understand and implement the principles of "multifunctional ships fleet" and "polymetric measurement" in their multivariate digital monitoring, decision-making support, and control systems development projects.

References

[1]   H. Lee, J. Romero. Climate Change 2023: Synthesis Report. Contribution of Working Groups I, II and III to the Sixth Assessment Report of the Intergovernmental Panel on Climate Change. IPCC, Geneva, Switzerland, pp. 1-34, doi:10.59327/IPCC/AR6-9789291691647.001https://www.ipcc.ch/report/ar6/syr/downloads/report/IPCC_AR6_SYR_SPM.pdf

[2]   P. Forster et al. The Earth's Energy Budget, Climate Feedbacks and Climate Sensitivity. Published online by Cambridge University Press: 29 June 2023, pp. 923-1054, doi: https://www.cambridge.org/core/services/aop-cambridge-core/content/view/AE57C97E588FF3060C7C7E47DD4F3C6E/stamped-9781009157889c7_923-1054.pdf/the-earths-energy-budget-climate-feedbacks-and-climate-sensitivity.pdf

[3]   K. Cios et al. Data Mining: Knowledge discovery approach. Springer Science+Busines Media, 2007, XV, 606 p.

[4]   I. Witten et al. Data Mining: Practical Machine Learning Tools and Techniques, Third Edition: Morgan Kaufman Series in Data Management Systems. Morgan Kaufman, 3 edit., 2011, 664 p.

[5]   I. Devici Kocakoc, M. Pulat. Evolution and Optimization in Machine Learning: A Bibliometric Analysis and Strategy Overview. Authorea. September 26, 2023. DOI:10.22541/au.169574593/30757767/v1.

[6]   EU AI Act: First regulation on artificial intelligence. European Parliament, August 2023. DOI: https://www.europarl.europa.eu/pdfs/news/expert/2023/6/story/20230601STO93804/20230601STO93804_en.pdf.Lastaccessed2024/01/31.

[7]   C. Stokel-Walker, R. Van Noorden, The promise and peril of generative AI, Nature 614, February 9, 2023, pp. 214-216.

[8]   X. Xu, Y. Lu et al. Industry 4.0 and Industry 5.0—inception, conception, and perception, J. Manuf. Syst., 61(October) (2021) 530-535. https://doi.org/10.1016/j.jmsy.2021.10.006.

[9]   K. Demir et al, The next industrial revolution: industry 5.0 and discussions on industry 4.0, Ind. 4.0 MIS Perspect., January 2019, pp. 247–260.

[10] A. George et al. The Evolution of Smart Factories: How Industry 5.0 is Revolutionizing Manufacturing. PUIRP Publications, 2023, pp. 33-53, doi: https://www.researchgate.net/publication/374921635_The_Evolution_of_Smart_Factories_How_Industry_50_is_Revolutionizing_Manufacturing

[11] Artificial Intelligence. Markets and Markets: Semiconductor & Electronics. doi: https://www.marketsandmarkets.com/Industry/semiconductor_and_electronics

[12] Artificial Intelligence. Markets and Markets: Information & Communication. doi: https://www.marketsandmarkets.com/Industry/information_and_communications_technology

[13] Artificial Intelligence. Markets and Markets: Automotive & Transportation. doi: https://www.marketsandmarkets.com/Industry/automotive_and_transportation

[14] Artificial Intelligence. Markets and Markets: Aerospace & Defense. doi: https://www.marketsandmarkets.com/Industry/aerospace_and_defence

[15] Artificial Intelligence. Markets and Markets: Energy & Power. doi: https://www.marketsandmarkets.com/Industry/energy_and_power

[16] Emergence of AI based business models. Mega Trends: Artificial Intelligence, Whitepaper M&M, 2023. doi: https://www.facebook.com/fimbape saro24/

[17] Shipbuilding: Global Analysis, Insights and Forecast, 2023-2030: Fortune Business Insights. doi: https://www.fortunebusinessinsights.com/

[18] K. Hossine et al. Metrology for 2020s. Middlesex, UK: National Physical Laboratory, 2012, 28 p.

[19] A. Hasan et al. Emerging Technologies in Digital Manufacturing and Smart Factories.? In Advances in Logistics, Operations, and Management Science, Book Series, IGI Global Publisher, January 2024, 313 p.

[20] A. García-Domínguez. Mobile Applications, Cloud and Bigdata on Ships and Shore Stations for Increased Safety on Marine Traffic; a Smart Ship Project. University of Tennessee, December 2023, UTC from IEEE Xplore, pp. 1532-1537.

[21] M. Myvizhi et al. Sustainable Supply Chain Management in the Age of Machine Intelligence: Addressing Challenges, Capitalizing on Opportunities, and Shaping the Future Landscape. SMIJ 2023, Vol. 3. https://doi.org/10.61185/SMIJ.2023.33103

[22] P. Centobelli, R. Cerchione et al. Sailing through a digital and resilient shipbuilding supply chain: An empirical investigation. Journal of Business Research, 2023, 13 p. https://doi.org/10.1016/j.jbusres.2023.113686

[23] A. Qazi, J. Quigley et al. Cost-Effectiveness and Manageability Based Prioritisation of Supply Chain Risk Mitigation Strategies. In: Supply Chain Risk Management. Springer, Singapore, 2018, pp. 23-42. https://doi.org/10.1007/978-981-10-4106-8_2

[24] A. K. Gupta, Framework for the selection of sustainable suppliers using integrated compensatory fuzzy AHP-TOPSIS multi-criteria approach. In: IEEE International Conference on Industrial Engineering and Engineering Management (IEEM), Kuala Lumpur, Malaysia, 2022, pp. 0772–0775. https://doi.org/10.1109/IEEM55944.2022.9989663.

[25] D. Hapishko, I. Sidenko, G. Kondratenko, Y. Zhukov, Y. Kondratenko, Modification of Fuzzy TOPSIS Based on Various Proximity Coefficients Metrics and Shapes of Fuzzy Sets. In: Antoniou, G. et al. Information and Communication Technologies in Education, Research, and Industrial Applications. ICTERI 2023. Communications 72 Multivariate Information Systems and Polymetric Sensors in Computer and Information Science, vol 1980. Springer, Cham, 2023, pp. 98-113. doi: https://doi.org/10.1007/978-3-031-48325-7_8

[26] Y. Kondratenko, S. Sidorenko, Ship Navigation in Narrowness Passes and Channels in Uncertain Conditions: Intelligent Decision Support. In: P. Shi et al. (Eds.), Complex Systems: Spanning Control and Computational Cybernetics: Foundations, volume 414 of Studies in Systems, Decision, and Control, vol. 414, Springer, Cham, 2022, pp. 475-493. https://doi.org/10.1007/978-3-030-99776-2_24

[27] V. Timchenko et al., Decision Support System for the Safety of Ship Navigation Based on Optical Color Logic Gates. CEUR Workshop Proceedings, Vol. 3347, 2022, pp. 42–52. 4th International Scientific Conference "Information Technology and Implementation," IT&I'2022, Virtual, Online, 30 Nov - 2 Dec 2022, 186836

[28] A. Cozar et al., 2014. Plastic Debris in the Open Ocean. University of Hawaii, Honolulu. PNAS. July 15, 2014, vol.111, no. 28, pp.10239–10244.

[29] J. Boucher et al. Primary Microplastics in the Oceans: A Global Evaluation of Sources. IUCN, Gland, Switzerland, 2017, 43 p.

[30] M. Eriksen et al. Plastic pollution in the world's oceans. PLOS ONE (Public Library of Science) 9 (12), e111913, 2014, pp. 1–15.

[31] E. Howell et al. On North Pacific circulation and associated marine debris concentration. Mar. Pollut. Bull. (65), 2012, pp. 16–22.

[32] N. Bellou et al. Global assessment of innovative solutions to tackle marine litter. Nature Sustainability, Vol 516, 4 June 2021, pp. 516–524. doi: https://doi.org/10.1038/s41893-021-00726-2

[33] E. Murphy et al. A decision framework for estimating the cost of marine plastic pollution interventions. Conservation Biology, 2021, pp. 1–11. https://doi.org/10.1111/cobi.13827

[34] S. Taffel. Communicative Capitalism, Technological Solutionism, and the Ocean Cleanup. In: Plastic Legacies. Pollution, Persistence, and Politics, AU Press, Athabasca University, 2021, pp. 181-202. doi: https://doi.org/10.15215/aupress/9781771993272.01

[35] I. Napper et al. Marine Litter: Are There Solutions to This Global Environmental Problem? In: Plastic Legacies. Pollution, Persistence, and Politics, AU Press, Athabasca University, 2021, pp. 25-40. doi: https://doi.org/10.15215/aupress/9781771993272.01

[36] A. van Giezen et al. Spoilt - Ocean Cleanup: Alternative logistics chains to accommodate plastic waste recycling: An economic evaluation. Transportation Research Interdisciplinary Perspectives, 5, 2020, pp. 1–12.

[37] Yu. Zhukov et al. OPUSS Project: First Results and Roadmap of Development. XII International Conference on Innovations in Shipbuilding and Ocean Technologies. National University of Shipbuilding, Mykolaiv, 30 Sept-01, Oct 2021, pp. 593-598.

[38] J. Hopewell et al. Plastics recycling: challenges and opportunities. Philos. Trans. R. Soc. London. Ser. B: Biol. Sci. V. 364 (1526), 2009, pp. 2115–2126.

[39]   Recycled carpeting: another way to support plastic recycling, 2010. [Online] at: https://www.plasticsmakeitpossible.com/plastics-recycling/howto-recycle/at-home/recycle-your-carpeting/, Accesseddate:31.01.2024.

[40]   The project of a special-purpose vessel for the collection and processing of plastic garbage polluting the waters of oceans, seas and lakes. PL421955 (A1), B63B35/32, published 13.08.2018.

[41]   Energy-saving apparatus for collecting and sorting large marine debris using a catamaran and a method for collecting and sorting large marine debris. WO2014038732 (A1), B09B3/00; B63B1/10; B63B35/32; E02B15/04, published 13.03.2014.

[42]   Device for collecting plastic waste from the water surface. WO2019073107 (A1), IPC V63V 35/32, Ye02V 15/00, publ. 18.04.2019.

[43]   Energy-saving apparatus for collecting and sorting large marine debris using a catamaran and a method for collecting and sorting large marine debris, PCT WO 2014191100 (A2), B63B 35/32, E02B 15/04, published 04.12.2014.

[44]   Catamaran vessel for plastic waste collection Scheme solution. Australian Patent Document AU2015100062 (A4), IPC B63B35/28; B63B35/32, publ. 26.02.2015.

[45]   Multifunctional vessel for collecting plastic waste. China Patent Document CN103921901 (A), IPC B63B35/32; E02B15/10, publ. 16.07.2014.

[46]   A mobile vessel for collecting micro-plastic waste and a way to collect micro-plastic waste. China Patent Document CN108725706 (A), IPC B63B35/32; E02B15/10; H02J7/35, publ. 02.11.2018.

[47]   Full surface two-hull vessel for collection of floating plastic particles. China Patent Document CN109591970 (A), IPC B63B1/10; B63B35/32; E02B15/10, publ. 09.04.2019.

[48]   Vessel for garbage collection. Japanese Patent Document JPS6343892 (A), IPC V63V 35/00, issue 24.02.1988.

[49]   Ship for recycling plastic waste. Korean Patent Document KR20150119993 (A), IPC B09B3/00; B63B35/32; B63J3/04; E02B15/10, issue 27.10.2015.

[50]   Y. Zhukov et al. System of vessels and/or floating structures for utilizing plastic waste polluting the world's oceans waters. PCT, WO2022260643 (A1), B63B25/04; B63B25/08; B63B35/32; E02B15/10, published — 2022-12-15.

[51]   Y. Zhukov et al. System of vessels and/or floating structures for utilizing plastic waste polluting the world's oceans waters. PCT, WO2022260644 (A1), B63B25/04; B63B25/08; B63B35/32; E02B15/10, published — 2022-12-15.

[52]   Y. Zhukov et al. Vessel or floating structure for utilizing plastic waste polluting the world's oceans waters. PCT, WO2022260645 (A1),

B63B25/04; B63B25/08; B63B35/32; E02B15/10, published — 2022-12-15.

[53]   M. Höyhtyä, J. Huusko et al. Connectivity for Autonomous Ships: Architecture, Use Cases, and Research Challenges. 8th International Conference on ICT Convergence, Jeju Island, Korea, October 2017. DOI: 10.1109/ICTC.2017.8191000.

[54]   M. Bakker et al. A model predictive control approach towards the energy efficiency of submerged dredging. Ocean Engineering, 287, [115770], 2023, 15 p. https://doi.org/10.1016/j.oceaneng.2023.115770.

[55]   Autonomous dredging requires over 60% less energy than conventional dredging. C-Job Naval Architects BV Web Site. https://c-job.com/wp-content/upl oads/2019/11/C-Job-AUMD-research-paper.pdf.Lastseen31.01.2024.

[56]   Uncrewed Surface Vessel. DEMCON Unmanned Systems. Online: https://demcon-unmanned.nl/cases/.Lastseen31.01.2024.

[57]   Global Level Gauge Market by Type (Tank Level Gauges, Fuel Level Gauges, Water Level Gauges, Mechanical Level Gauges), by Technology (Magnetic, Reflexive, Transparent, Others), by End-user Industry Oil and Gas, Chemical, Water Treatment, Marine, Others): Global Opportunity Analysis and Industry Forecast, 2021-2031. 250 p. – Available at URL: https://www.alliedmarketresearch.com/level-gauge-market.Lastseen31.01.2024.

[58]   Y. Kondratenko, et al., Slip displacement sensors for intelligent robots: Solutions and models, in: Proceedings of the 2013 IEEE 7th International Conference on Intelligent Data Acquisition and Advanced Computing Systems, IDAACS 2013, vol. 2, art. no. 6663050, 2013, pp. 861-866. doi: 10.1109/IDAACS.2013.6663050.

[59]   A. Topalov, G. Kondratenko, O. Gerasin, O. Kozlov, O., Zivenko, Information system for automatic planning of liquid ballast distribution, Proceedings of the 2nd International Workshop on Information Communication Technologies & Embedded Systems (ICTES 2020), Mykolaiv, Ukraine, CEUR Workshop Proceedings, Vol. 2762, 2020, pp. 191-200. http://ceur-ws.org/Vol-2762/paper13.pdf

[60]   Y. Zhukov et al. Polymetric sensing of intelligent robots, 2013 IEEE 7th International Conference on Intelligent Data Acquisition and Advanced Computing Systems (IDAACS), 2013, pp. 880-884, DOI: https://doi.org/10.1109/IDAACS.2013.6663053.

[61]   Yu. Zhukov et al. Intelligent Polymetric Systems Industrial Applications / Proceedings of the 2nd International Workshop on Information-Communication Technologies & Embedded Systems (ICTES 2020) Mykolaiv, Ukraine, 2020, pp. 122-137. http://ceur-ws.org/Vol-2762/paper8.pdf.

[62]   O. Zivenko et al. Level measurement principles & sensors. II Materialy IX mezinárodni vedecko-prackticka conference "Veda a technologie: krok do budoucnosti - 2013". - Dil. 28. Technicke vdy. Prague, 2013, pp. 85-90.

[63] Zivenko O. LPG accounting specificity during its storage and transportation // Measuring Equipment and Metrology, Issue No3 (80), 2019, pp. 21-27. https://doi.org/10.23939/istcmtm2019.03.021.

[64] Y. Kondratenko et al., Machine Learning Techniques for Increasing Efficiency of the Robot's Sensor and Control Information Processing, Sensors 2022, 22(3), 1062. doi: 10.3390/s22031062.

[65] R. Boute et al. AI in Logistics and Supply Chain Management. In Global Logistics and Supply Chain Strategies for the 2020s: Vital Skills for the Next Generation, Springer, 2022, pp. 49–65.

[66] K. Czachorowski, M. Solesvik, Y. Kondratenko, 'The Application of Blockchain Technology in the Maritime Industry,' Studies in Systems, Decision and Control, vol 171, Springer, Cham, 2019, pp. 561-577. DOI: https://doi.org/10.1007/978-3-030-00253-4_24.

Authors' Short CV

Yuriy Zhukov graduated from Mykolaiv Shipbuilding Institute in 1974 with a Naval Architect degree. Candidate of Sciences in Ship Design and Engineering from 1981. Associated Professor and Chief of the NSI academic research department from 1982 to 1990. Chief of Maritime Instrumentation Chair at the Admiral Makarov National University of Shipbuilding from 1993. Doctor of Sciences (Tech.), Professor. Laureate of State Award of Ukraine in Science and Technology. Honored Inventor of Ukraine. Author of the axiomatic theory of polymetric measurements.

Oleksii Zivenko obtained his Bachelor's and master's degrees at Admiral Makarov National University of Shipbuilding in 2007 and 2009. He earned a Ph.D. in Computer Systems and Components from Petro Mohyla Black Sea University in 2013. Assistant Professor of Marine Instrumentation Department at Admiral Makarov National University. Research focuses on sensory systems for simultaneous measurements of various physical quantities, optimizing high-precision experiments, automating data analysis, and reducing uncertainties.

4

There is Still Plenty of Room at the Bottom: Feynman's Vision of Quantum Computing 65 Years Later

---

Alexis Lupo[1], Olga Kosheleva[1], Vladik Kreinovich[1],
Victor Timchenko[2], and Yuriy Kondratenko[3]

[1]University of Texas at El Paso, El Paso, Texas, USA
[2]Admiral Makarov National University of Shilbuilding, Mykolaiv, Ukraine
[3]Black Sea State University named after Petro Mohyla
Mykolaiv, Ukraine, and Institute of Artificial Intelligence Problems
of MES and NAS of Ukraine, Kyiv, Ukraine
Email: alupo@miners.utep.edu, olgak@utep.edu, vladik@utep.edu
vl.timchenko58@gmail.com, y_kondrat2002@yahoo.com

Abstract

In 1959, Nobelist Richard Feynman gave a talk titled "There's plenty of room at the bottom", in which he emphasized that, to drastically speed up computations, we need to make computer components much smaller – all the way to the size of molecules, atoms, and even elementary particles. At this level, physics is no longer described by deterministic Newton's mechanics, it is described by probabilistic quantum laws. Because of this, computer designers started thinking about how to design a reliable computer based on non-deterministic elements – and this thinking eventually led to the modern ideas and algorithms of quantum computing. So, we have a straight path of speeding up computations: by learning how to use molecules, atoms, and then elementary particles as building blocks of a computational device. But what if we reach the size of an elementary particle? At first glance, it may seem that we will then reach an absolute limit of how fast a computer can be. However, as we show in this paper, we can potentially speed up computations even further – by using the internal structure of elementary particles, e.g., the fact that protons and neutrons consist of quarks. Interestingly, the corresponding mathematics is very similar to what is called color optical computing – the use of light of different colors in computations.

Keywords: Faster computers, Feynman, quantum computing, color optical computing, quarks.

4.1 Introduction

Computers are very fast. Computers now are several orders of magnitude faster then a few decades ago. An average laptop – like the one on which we type this text – performs 4 billion operations per second, much more than record-breaking supercomputers a few decades ago.

A simple calculator has more computing power in it than all the computers that supported the 1960s going-to-the-Moon Apollo program.

But not fast enough. In spite of all these successes, one of the main challenges that computing faces is that for many practical applications, the current computer speed is not sufficient. The media is full of descriptions of how the speed of current high performance computers limits our ability to further improve Large Language Models like the famous ChatGPT.

But to explain the need for faster computing, one does not have to cite such futuristic examples: the need for faster computing is ubiquitous in many real-time control applications, where we need to make control decisions really fast; see, e.g., [1, 4].

How can we further speed up computers? Engineers working on computer design focus on specific *technical* issues, e.g., how to minimize the undesirable interactions between two neighboring transistors. But, in addition to technical issues, there are also *fundamental* issues that make speeding up computers difficult. One such issue is the fact that, according to special relativity theory (see, e.g., [3, 6]) information cannot be transferred faster than the speed of light.

It is easy to see that this limitation directly affects the computer speed. For example, the laptop on which we type this text has a diagonal size of about

30 cm: this is the largest distance between the two points from the laptop. If we divide 30 cm by the speed of light – which is approximately 300 000 km/s – we can conclude that it takes at least 1 nanosecond for a signal to go between these two points. During this time, our 4 GHz laptop has already performed four operations. So, a natural conclusion is that if we want to make computers faster, we need to make computers smaller in size – and this, in turn, means that all the computer components must be made smaller. And this is exactly the tendency that computer designers have been following.

Feynman's 1959 talk. Nobel-winning physicist Richard Feynman was the first who, in his famous 1959 talk titled "There's plenty of room at the bottom" [2], explained the natural consequences of this need for miniaturization. According to Feynman, since we need to have smaller and smaller components to design faster and faster computers, eventually we will have to decrease the size of these components to sizes comparable with the sizes of individual molecules.

And here comes an important challenge. At the usual macro-level – in particular, at component sizes that were prevalent at that time – the vast majority of events in the computing process can be described by Newton's mechanics. One of the important features of Newton's mechanics is that it is deterministic: once we know the initial state, we can uniquely predict all future states. A good illustration of this determinism is celestial mechanics, the first area to which Newton applied his mechanics: we can predict Solar eclipses hundreds years ahead, and what we observe now, in the 21 century, is in perfect accordance with predictions made several centuries ago.

This determinism is a perfect fit for what we want for computer components: we want computers to perform the same sequence of computations every time we need it, we do not want to have different answers to the same computational problem. And here lies a challenge. Already molecules – and even more atoms and elementary particles – cannot be fully described by Newtonian physics. To adequately describe the behavior of molecules, atoms, and elementary particles, we need to use quantum physics; see, e.g., [3, 6]. And one of the features of quantum physics is that it is non-deterministic: we cannot predict what exactly will happen in the future, we can only predict the *probabilities* of different futures. For example, if we take an atom of a radioactive material such as uranium (U), we cannot predict when exactly it will decay – we can only compute the probability that it will decay before a given moment of time.

So Feynman formulated a challenge to computer designers: once components reach the size at which quantum effects need to be taken into account, how can we design a deterministic reliable computer out of such non-deterministic unreliable elements?

Feynman's idea eventually led to modern quantum computing. When a Nobel prize winner talks, people listen. So researchers started thinking about how a reliable computer can be built from quantum components. And they succeeded, even beyond Feynman's original expectations: not only quantum algorithms lead to a deterministic answer, some of these algorithms are actually much faster than the corresponding deterministic ones – so, in addition to a speedup caused by a decrease in size, we have an additional speedup caused by using quantum physics. Here are the two classical examples (for details, see, e.g., [5]).

The first example is searching for an element with the desired property in an unsorted list. If we have a list with n elements then, in a non-quantum world, the only thing you can do is search the elements one by one. If you are in luck, you can find the desired element at the very first attempt. However, no matter in what order you test these elements, in the worst case, the last element you search is the desired one. So, in the worst case, the time needed for this search is proportional to the number of elements n. Interestingly, by using quantum effects, Lov Grover came up with an algorithm that requires, in the worst case, time proportional to the square root of n – which is, of course, much faster. For example, in the case we have a million records, we have $\sqrt{n} = 1000$, so the search time decreases by a factor of thousand.

The second example is a fast quantum algorithm developed by Peter Shor for factoring large integers. This may sound like a not-very-useful theoretical problem, but it is actually very practically important, since most current encryption algorithms for computer-based communications are based on the understanding that factoring large integers is very complex. For example, the most widely used RSA algorithm uses a product $n = p_1 \cdot p_2$ of two large prime numbers p_1 and p_2 for encoding.

- If one knows the values p_1 and p_2, then decoding is easy.
- However, in situations when we do not know the factors, when we know only their product, all known non-quantum algorithms require unrealistic astronomical time to decode.

In contrast, Shor's quantum algorithm finds the factors in feasible time – provided, of course, that we have a universal quantum computer with a sufficient number of quantum bits (also known as *qubits*). This may not be the most interesting application of quantum computing, but the possibility to be able to read all secret messages is the main reason why many governments invest billions of dollars in quantum computing research.

Limits to growth. This all sounds good: we can go from using molecules as computational elements to using atoms to using elementary particles – and each time we drastically decrease the size of computing elements, we drastically speed up computations.

But there seems to be a limit; once we reach the level of elementary particles, there is no way to go. By definition, elementary particles are the end in itself, they cannot be divided into smaller parts. In Feynman's words, once we reach the level of elementary particles, there seems to be no remaining room at the bottom.

So what can we do?

There is still plenty of room at the bottom: what we do in this paper. In this paper, we show that, contrary to the above first impression, it *is* potentially possible to further speed up computations. In other words, we will show that there is still plenty of room at the bottom.

4.2 Our Idea

Let us recall some physics: the basic facts about quarks. To explain our idea, we need to recall basic facts about such elementary particles as protons and neutrons; see, e.g., [3, 6].

Yes, as we have mentioned earlier, these are elementary particles:

- We can divide an atom into electrons, protons, and neutrons
- But we cannot divide a proton or a neutron into smaller particles.

On the other hand, we all have read in popular articles that protons and neutrons consist of special particles called *quarks*. It is important to understand that this "consists of" has a different meaning that a similar statement that an atom consists of elementary particles:

- An atom *can* be divided into elementary particles
- But a proton or neutron *cannot* be divided into quarks.

We can actually observe quarks by experiment similar to what Rutherford did at the dawn of atomic physics to show that an atom consists of a nucleus and other particles floating in empty space. When he bombarded a layer of material with energetic alpha-particles, in most cases, they went through or deviated a little bit, but in some cases, they were reflected almost 180° and moved back. This showed that most of the space in a solid body is practically empty, but there are few areas with high concentration of matter that lead to a strong reflection.

Similarly, if we bombard protons with high-energy particles, there are a few cases when we get a very strong reaction. This shows, kind of, that inside a proton there are dense areas – known as *partons* – surrounded by (almost) empty space. These partons is what physicists call *quarks*. A proton or a neutron consists of three quarks. (It should be mentioned that there are other particles – e.g., pions, responsible for strong interactions – that consist of two quarks.)

Just like a nucleus forms a very small part of the corresponding atom, partons occupy a very small part of the particle. In this sense, the partons (quarks) are very small, much smaller than elementary particles themselves.

In contrast to particles in an atom – that can be separated – quarks cannot be separated from each other. The possibility to separate elementary particles from each other is based on the fact that for interactions between these particles – be they electromagnetic interactions or "strong" interactions between protons and neutrons – the interaction force decreases with distance. So, once we apply some energy and move the particles sufficiently far away from each other, it is sufficient to apply a relatively small force and separate them completely.

In contrast, as experiments showed, if we try to increase the distance between quarks, the force pushing them back does not decrease at all. So, no matter how far away we move them apart, they will still be connected as forcefully as before.

Quark colors. The observed interaction between quarks seems to imply that each flavor of quarks can be of three different types (and an anti-quark can be of one of the opposite types), so that an elementary particle:

- Either has three quarks of different types
- Or has three anti-quarks of different anti-types
- Or has a quark of some type and an anti-quark of the corresponding anti-type.

Physicists observed that this is somewhat similar to three basic colors: red (R), green (G), and blue (B), with anti-colors interpreted as filters stopping the corresponding color. In this interpretation, the only way to avoid colors – and to get white or black – is:

- Either to combine all three colors
- Or to apply all three filters
- Or to combine a single color with the corresponding filter.

So, there is a natural analogy between quark types and colors, in which elementary particles – formed by quarks – cannot have color, they have to be black or white.

Because of this analogy, quark types are usually called *colors* – but it is important remember that beyond this simple analogy, quark types have nothing to do with the actual basic colors – which correspond to electromagnetic waves of certain frequencies.

So how can we potentially use quarks for computations? Quarks are smaller than elementary particles. So if we can use quarks for computations, we can definitely speed up computations. But how can we do it?

How can we use any device for computations? Performing computations means changing some states. So, to be useful for computing, an object has to have at least two different states – otherwise, if the object has only one possible state, we cannot do anything with it. The simplest case is when we have exactly two different states. This way, we can use this object to represent a bit; we associate one of its states with 0, and another states with 1. If an object has more than two states, we may be able to use it to represent 2 or more bits.

From this viewpoint, let us consider two states of each of the three quarks that form a proton or a neutron: a usual state and an excited state. Then, depending on which of three quarks are excited, we get the following eight different options – which we will describe by the combination of colors of excited quarks:

- It may be that none of the quarks is excited; in terms of the color analogy, this corresponds to black; we will denote this proton state by B.
- It may be that only the red quark is excited; we will denote this proton state by R.
- It may be that only the green quark is excited; we will denote this proton state by G.
- It may be that only the blue quark is excited; we will denote this proton state by B.
- It may be that only red and green quarks are excited; we will denote this proton state by R + G.

- It may be that only red and blue quarks are excited; we will denote this proton state by R + B.
- It may be that only blue and green quarks are excited; we will denote this proton state by G + B.
- It may be that all three quarks are excited; in terms of the color analogy, this corresponds to white; we will denote this proton state by W.

In our analogy, states of anti-proton correspond to similar filters. Mixing of the two colors means that the two protons interact, so that one of them stops being excited and the excitation energy moves to the other proton.

This becomes very similar to color optical computing. At first glance, the above scheme sounds very complex, and it is not immediately clear what we can do with these eight states. The good news is that this has already been studied for actual colors, namely, several schemes have been proposed to use combinations of basic colors for computations (see, e.g., [7, 8, 9, 10, 11, 12]) – and some of these schemes turned to be useful for such practical tasks as providing safety of ship navigation [8].

So, our idea is to apply this computational scheme to quark colors.

4.3 Conclusion

No matter how fast our computers have become, there is still a practical need for faster computations. To speed up computations, we need to make computer components smaller in size. In 1959, exactly 65 years ago, Nobel-winning physicist Richard Feynman presented a talk titled "There's plenty of room at the bottom" (published in 1960), in which he explored this idea and predicted that eventually, we will have to bring the size of our components to the size of molecules – and then atoms and elementary particles. To do that, said Feynman, we need to take into account that at these sizes, Nature follows not deterministic Newton's laws, but probabilistic laws of quantum physics. So, we need to think how to perform deterministic computations on a computer consisting of such non-deterministic components. Computer researchers solved this challenge – and Feynman's 1960 paper is now considered one of the foundational papers of the field of quantum computing, with all its spectacular theoretical (and potentially practical) successes.

This is all good, but as we progress in this direction, we seem to hit a limit to the possible computer speed up: we will get a drastic speedup when we get to the level of atoms and then elementary particles, but after that, there seems to be nowhere to go, there seems to be no room left at the bottom.

In this paper, we show that we *can* go further, we *can* potentially achieve further speedup, that there is still plenty of room at the bottom. Specifically, we show that:

- While we cannot divide an elementary particle like proton or neuron into smaller parts
- We *can* use the fact that, in some reasonable sense, a proton and a neutron consist of three "sub-particles" – quarks.

While these sub-particles cannot be separated, they have a certain autonomy within a proton or a neutron.

We propose to use this autonomy and thus, to use quarks for computations – since quarks are smaller than the elementary particles formed from them, this will potentially lead to an additional computational speedup.

Interestingly, because of the known analogy between quark types and basic colors – because of which quark types are called quark colors – the quark-based resulting computational environment is similar to the computational environment of color optical computing, when we use light of different colors for computations. We can therefore use computational techniques from color optical computing for quark computations as well.

Acknowledgments

This work was supported in part by the National Science Foundation grants 1623190 (A Model of Change for Preparing a New Generation for Professional Practice in Computer Science), HRD-1834620 and HRD-2034030 (CAHSI Includes), EAR-2225395 (Center for Collective Impact in Earthquake Science C-CIES), and by the AT&T Fellowship in Information Technology.

It was also supported by a grant from the Hungarian National Research, Development and Innovation Office (NRDI).

References

[1]   R. Duro and Y. Kondratenko (Eds.), *Advances in Intelligent Robotics and Collaborative Automation*, River Publishers, Aalborg, Denmark, 2015.

[2]   R. Feynman, "There's plenty of room at the bottom", *Engineering and Science*, 1960. Vol. 23, No. 5, pp. 22–36.

[3]   R. Feynman, R. Leighton, and M. Sands, *The Feynman Lectures on Physics*, Addison Wesley, Boston, Massachusetts, 2005.

[4]   V. M. Kuntsevich, V. F. Gubarev, Y. P. Kondratenko, D. V. Lebedev, and V. P. Lysenko (Eds.), *Control Systems: Theory and Applications*, River Publishers, Gistrup, Denmark, and Delft, Netherlands, 2018.

[5]   M. A. Nielsen and I. L. Chuang, *Quantum Computation and Quantum Information*, Cambridge University Press, Cambridge, U.K., 2011.

[6]   K. S. Thorne and R. D. Blandford, *Modern Classical Physics: Optics, Fluids, Plasmas, Elasticity, Relativity, and Statistical Physics*, Princeton University Press, Princeton, New Jersey, 2021.

[7]   V. Timchenko, Yu. Kondratenko, O. Kozlov, and V. Kreinovich, "Fuzzy color computing based on optical logical architecture", *Lecture Notes in Networks and Systems*, 2023, Vol. 758, pp. 491–498.

[8]   V. Timchenko, Yu. Kondratenko, and V. Kreinovich, "Decision support system for the safety of ship navigation based on optical color logic gates", *CEUR Workshop Proceedings*, 2022, Vol. 3347, pp. 42–52.

[9]   V. Timchenko, Yu. Kondratenko, and V. Kreinovich, "The architecture of optical logical coloroid with fuzzy computing", *CEUR Workshop Proceedings*, 2023, Vol. 3373, pp. 638–648.

[10]   V. Timchenko, Yu. Kondratenko, and V. Kreinovich, "Implementation of optical logic gates based on color filters", *Lecture Notes on Data Engineering and Communications Technologies*, 2023, 181, pp. 126–136.

[11]   V. Timchenko, Yu. Kondratenko, and V. Kreinovich, "Interval-valued and set-valued extensions of discrete fuzzy logics, Belnap logic, and color optical computing", *Springer Lecture Notes in Computer Science*, 2023, Vol. 14069, pp. 297–303.

[12]   V. Timchenko, Yu. Kondratenko, and V. Kreinovich, "Why color optical computing?", *Springer Studies in Computational Intelligence*, 2023, Vol. 1097, pp. 227–233.

Decision Support System for Maintenance Planning of Vortex Electrostatic Precipitators Based on IoT and AI Techniques

Lu Congxiang[1], Oleksiy Kozlov[2,*], Galyna Kondratenko[2], and Anna Aleksieieva[2]

[1]Yancheng Polytechnic College, Yancheng, China
[2]Petro Mohyla Black Sea National University, Mykolaiv, Ukraine
Email: lucongxiang@126.com, kozlov_ov@ukr.net,
halyna.kondratenko@chmnu.edu.ua, anna.aleksyeyeva@chmnu.edu.ua
*Corresponding Author

Abstract

This research addresses the issue of introducing an intelligent decision support system (DSS) for efficient maintenance planning of vortex electrostatic precipitators (VEPs) in industrial settings. Leveraging the integration of Internet of Things (IoT) and artificial intelligence (AI) techniques, the proposed DSS aims to significantly reduce equipment downtime through the optimization of cleaning modes and schedules. In light of the increasing importance of production efficiency and continuous improvement of intelligent technologies, this study becomes particularly relevant as it offers a comprehensive solution for optimizing VEP performance using AI. The intelligent DSS, created based on a hierarchical approach and utilizing two fuzzy subsystems, proves to be a valuable tool, providing operators with essential recommendations based on real-time VEP conditions. By dynamically adjusting cleaning parameters, including intensity, duration, and time until mandatory cleaning, the system demonstrates adaptability and efficiency in maintenance planning, contributing to sustained reliability and effectiveness of VEPs in diverse industrial environments.

Keywords: Fuzzy decision support system; artificial intelligence; Internet of Things; vortex electrostatic precipitator; maintenance planning.

5.1 Introduction

Decision support systems (DSSs) play a pivotal role in modern organizational structures, serving as indispensable tools for efficient decision-making [1]. Their importance spans across various fields, contributing to the effectiveness of managerial and operational processes [2, 3]. A DSS aids decision-makers by providing them with organized and relevant information, thereby assisting in problem-solving and strategic planning. The dynamic nature of these systems allows decision-makers to interact with data, perform analyses, and generate insights, fostering a more informed and agile decision-making environment [4].

In diverse fields such as engineering, business, healthcare, finance, and logistics, decision support systems have become integral components of day-to-day operations [5–7]. They contribute to streamlined workflows, enhanced data management, and improved overall efficiency. By facilitating the processing of large datasets and offering analytical tools, a DSS empowers decision-makers to navigate complex scenarios, anticipate trends, and respond proactively to challenges. The constant and intensive development of DSSs reflects the evolving needs of organizations in an ever-changing landscape. As technology advances, these systems continue to incorporate new features, improved interfaces, and more sophisticated analytical capabilities. The goal is to provide decision-makers with robust and user-friendly tools that align with the demands of the contemporary business environment, ultimately contributing to better decision outcomes and organizational success.

Currently, artificial intelligence methods serve as the foundation for a diverse range of DSSs, each contributing unique strengths to problem-solving in different domains [8, 9]. Fuzzy logic-based DSSs, drawing inspiration from human reasoning, excel in handling uncertainty and imprecision [10]. These systems leverage linguistic variables and rule-based reasoning, making them particularly valuable in environments characterized by ambiguity. In turn, neural network-based DSSs, inspired by the structure of the human brain, specialize in pattern recognition and complex data processing [11]. They prove effective for tasks such as predictive modeling, classification, and optimization, adapting and improving their performance over time through autonomous learning from data. Hybrid neuro-fuzzy networks represent a convergence of fuzzy logic and neural networks, offering a balanced approach to decision support and modeling [12]. This integration combines the interpretability and rule-based reasoning of fuzzy systems with the learning capabilities of neural networks, proving effective in dynamic systems that evolve over time.

Moreover, bio-inspired algorithms have proven to be quite effective in creating intelligent decision support systems [13]. Evolutionary algorithms, inspired by natural selection, optimize parameters and structures within these systems [14]. Swarm intelligence methods, drawing inspiration from the collective behavior of social animals and insects, find applications in DSS development, as well as optimize decision-making through simulated collaboration among individuals [15].

In addition, the integration of AI-driven DSSs with the Internet of Things creates intelligent, interconnected systems that can optimize processes in real-time [16, 17]. These approaches collectively enhance the adaptability, efficiency, and accuracy of AI-driven decision support across various sectors. The field remains dynamic, with ongoing exploration and development of algorithms and methodologies to further refine and expand the capabilities of decision support systems.

Along with various areas of application, special emphasis should be placed on the utilization of decision support systems in the management of intricate technological processes [18–20]. In particular, this work examines the development of an intelligent DSS for such a specialized area as operation and maintenance of vortex electrostatic precipitators. In turn, VEPs stand as crucial components across various industries, efficiently mitigating airborne particulate matter from industrial emissions and promoting environmental compliance [21–23]. The intricacies in managing VEPs arise from the complex electrostatic principles they employ and the necessity for adaptive control systems capable of handling diverse operational scenarios. A key challenge in maintaining optimal VEP performance lies in the careful upkeep of the system, particularly in timely cleaning [21]. The accumulation of deposited particles over time poses a significant threat to the precipitator's efficiency, impacting air quality control objectives and leading to increased energy consumption and operational costs. Recognizing the importance of routine and effective cleaning is paramount in sustaining the longevity and effectiveness of VEPs [22]. Industries must prioritize a comprehensive approach to maintenance, acknowledging the critical role cleaning plays in ensuring consistent, reliable performance and upholding environmental standards.

For now, various intelligent control systems have been devised for the operation of vortex electrostatic precipitators, including those with the implementation of fuzzy logic principles [24–26]. Despite these advancements, the challenge of establishing an efficient system to determine maintenance periods and modes for VEPs persists. Therefore, this study focuses on the creation of an intelligent decision support system for the maintenance planning of VEPs, leveraging Internet of Things and artificial intelligence techniques. The implementation of this intelligent DSS aims to reduce equipment downtime by optimizing cleaning modes and schedules, which will accordingly elevate the overall production efficiency across enterprises.

The subsequent sections of this chapter are structured as follows. Section 2 intricately outlines a comprehensive IoT-based hierarchical system designed for the remote monitoring and control of vortex electrostatic precipitators within an enterprise. Subsequently, Section 3 outlines the development process of the intelligent decision support system tailored for the maintenance planning of VEPs. Ultimately, Section 4 encapsulates concluding remarks and delineates potential directions for future research endeavors.

5.2 IoT-based Hierarchical System for Remote Monitoring and Control of Vortex Electrostatic Precipitators in an Enterprise

The development of the IoT-based hierarchical system is crucial for advancing the remote monitoring and control capabilities of vortex electrostatic precipitators. This advanced system must not only facilitate effective control but also enable remote adjustments and optimization of local-level control devices. The hierarchical structure ensures seamless communication between different levels, allowing for real-time data exchange and automatic control. By incorporating IoT technologies, this system aims to enhance the overall efficiency of VEPs by providing operators with the ability to remotely manage and fine-tune control parameters, optimizing the performance of these critical air purification devices in industrial environments.

In addition to its control functionalities, the IoT-based hierarchical system designed for VEPs must also possess robust diagnostic capabilities for real-time assessment. Remote collection of vital parameters regarding the condition of vortex electrostatic precipitators is essential for proactive maintenance and troubleshooting. In particular, it should incorporate a specialized remote decision support system based on AI techniques that analyzes the collected data and issues timely recommendations to operators regarding the necessity of maintenance activities. This comprehensive approach ensures that VEPs are not only controlled and optimized remotely but are also continuously monitored and supported through advanced diagnostic and decision-making features, ultimately contributing to enhanced operational reliability and longevity.

Hence, the configuration of the proposed IoT-based hierarchical system for remote monitoring and control of VEPs in an enterprise is illustrated in Figure 5.1, featuring the utilization of the following abbreviations: UCL is the upper control level; LCL is the lower control level; VEPi is the ith vortex electrostatic precipitator, which is installed in the ith workroom WRi (i = 1, 2, …, n); CDi is the ith control device for the ith VEP at the lower control level; WDTDi is the ith wireless data transmission device for the ith CD; $\mathbf{U}_{Vi}$ is the vector of the control signals of the ith VEP produced by its CD; $\mathbf{Y}_{Ri}$ is the vector of air parameters in the ith workroom, measured using appropriate sensors (not shown in Figure 5.1); $\mathbf{Y}_{Vi}$ is the vector of the ith VEP's parameters, measured using appropriate sensors (not shown in Figure 5.1); $\mathbf{X}_{CDi}$ is the vector of adjustable parameters of the ith control device; $\mathbf{Y}_R$ is the vector of measured

Figure 5.1: Configuration of the generalized IoT-based hierarchical system for remote monitoring and control of VEPs in an enterprise.

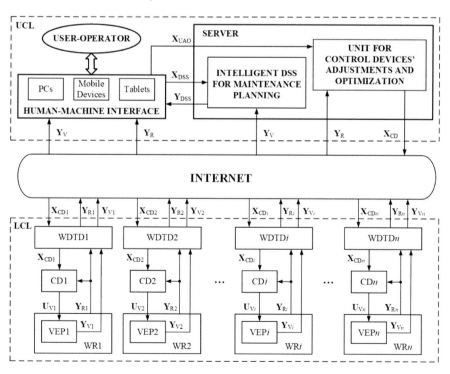

air parameters of all n workrooms ($\mathbf{Y}_R = \mathbf{Y}_{R1}, \mathbf{Y}_{R2}, ..., \mathbf{Y}_{Ri}, ..., \mathbf{Y}_{Rn}$); $\mathbf{Y}_V$ is the vector of measured parameters of all n VEPs ($\mathbf{Y}_V = \mathbf{Y}_{V1}, \mathbf{Y}_{V2}, ..., \mathbf{Y}_{Vi}, ..., \mathbf{Y}_{Vn}$); $\mathbf{X}_{CD}$ is the vector of adjustable parameters of all n CDs ($\mathbf{X}_{CD} = \mathbf{X}_{CD1}, \mathbf{X}_{CD2}, ..., \mathbf{X}_{CDi}, ..., \mathbf{X}_{CDn}$); $\mathbf{X}_{UAO}$ is the vector of customizable parameters of the unit for control devices' adjustments and optimization, which are set by the operator; $\mathbf{X}_{DSS}$ is the vector of customizable parameters of the decision support system for maintenance planning, which are set by the operator; $\mathbf{Y}_{DSS}$ is the vector of parameters that determine the DSS's recommendations for the operator regarding the necessary maintenance (cleaning) of VEPs.

The provided IoT-based hierarchical system is crafted to enable remote monitoring and control of n VEPs within an enterprise, ensuring their proper operation and timely maintenance. To receive feedback when controlling VEPs, certain sensors (not shown in the diagram) are employed to gauge the air pollution level (vector of measured air parameters $\mathbf{Y}_R$) in the workroom. In turn, at the lower control level, control devices (CDs) are utilized to facilitate the autonomous and high-performance control of VEPs. These controllers, depending on the current air pollution in the workrooms, regulate the required values of the air flow rate at the VEPs inlets and the voltage at their electrodes. Moreover, a number of other sensors (not shown in the diagram) are used for realization of the acquisition of information about the current state of VEPs themselves to further determine the required modes and duration of maintenance. To do this, it is necessary to measure the following VEPs' parameters: the number of deposited particles on the precipitator plates (particle deposition), the speed of the inlet air flow, the concentration of particles and the particle sizes. The data collected by all sensors (vectors $\mathbf{Y}_R$ and $\mathbf{Y}_V$) are transmitted to the upper control level through the Internet using wireless data transmission devices. Simultaneously, these devices receive the adjustable parameters of all n CDs from the upper control level denoted as the vector $\mathbf{X}_{CD}$.

The unit for control devices' adjustments and optimization is situated on a robust server, intended for executing modifications and structural-parametric optimization of CDs using advanced intelligent techniques when efficiency improvements are necessary during operation. Specifically, this facility can employ diverse methods such as evolutionary and multi-agent optimization [14, 15, 27]. In this context, the unit receives essential commands (vector $\mathbf{X}_{UAO}$) from the user-operator regarding the need to reconfigure and optimize specific CDs. To establish communication between the user-operator and the server, and to facilitate remote control and monitoring, a dedicated human–machine interface (HMI) is employed. This HMI is compatible with personal computers (PCs), tablets, and various mobile devices.

In turn, the intelligent decision support system for maintenance planning is also housed on a powerful server. Its main purpose is to analyze the current state of VEPs based on signals received from sensors (measuring particle deposition, flow speed, particle concentration, and particle sizes), as well as to generate pertinent recommendations for the operator concerning the required maintenance actions. Herewith, the DSS gives the operator the necessary recommendations for maintenance in the form of the vector $\mathbf{Y}_{\mathrm{DSS}}$. At the same time, the operator, for his part, can carry out all the various settings of the DSS by sending it customizable parameters in the form of the vector $\mathbf{X}_{\mathrm{DSS}}$.

Due to the advanced hierarchical structure introduced, this IoT-based system efficiently handles a large number of VEPs within an enterprise by utilizing only one optimization unit and only one DSS placed at the upper control level. These centralized units possess the capability to seamlessly transition from one VEP to another, ensuring the implementation of essential optimization measures and making informed decisions regarding necessary maintenance tasks. Therefore, this DSS is universal and can be used to determine the modes and duration of maintenance for VEPs of various capacities installed in workrooms with various area. For this purpose, input signals from sensors (particle deposition, flow speed, particle concentration, and particle sizes), as well as output signals corresponding to the necessary maintenance recommendations, are normalized and converted into relative units.

Moreover, this DSS can be built on the basis of various AI methods, in particular fuzzy logic, neural networks or neuro-fuzzy networks [10–12]. In this study, it is proposed to implement this system based on fuzzy logic, which will allow creating a flexible and easily customizable knowledge base, without the need for preliminary accumulation and processing of large volumes of experimental data. Thus, the next section presents the development of the fuzzy decision support system for the VEPs' maintenance planning.

5.3 Development of the Decision Support System for the VEPs' Maintenance Planning Based on Fuzzy Logic

To implement the planning of VEPs' maintenance modes, the input variables of the proposed fuzzy DSS are the following quantities: particle deposition D_{P}, flow speed V_{F}, particle concentration C_{P}, and particle sizes S_{P}. Herewith, these input quantities can be measured using the electrostatic dust sensors, differential pressure sensors, optical particle counters, and laser diffraction sensor, respectively. In turn, as for the DSS's outputs, the following variables are selected, which characterize the cleaning (maintenance) process: cleaning intensity I_C, cleaning duration T_C, and remaining time until cleaning T_R. Thus, the DSS's vectors of input $\mathbf{Y}_V$ and output $\mathbf{Y}_{DSS}$ variables are determined by the expressions:

$$\mathbf{Y}_V = \{D_P, V_F, C_P, S_P\} ; \tag{5.1}$$

$$\mathbf{Y}_{DSS} = \{I_C, T_C, T_R\} . \tag{5.2}$$

Herewith, the output variables of this system represent recommendations for the operator regarding the necessary maintenance (cleaning) of a certain VEP, depending on its current state (contamination) and its possible change in the near future. The first two variables indicate with what intensity and for how long it will be necessary to clean this VEP if cleaning begins immediately at this current moment. The third variable shows the remaining time until mandatory cleaning, if it is not already carried out at the moment. Thus, based on the recommendations received, the operator can easily decide whether it is worth initiating maintenance of this particular VEP at the moment, or whether it is better to wait some more time.

Since the proposed DSS has four inputs, even when using small numbers of linguistic term AI for each input variable, the rule base (RB) of this system will already have a fairly large number of rules (the number of rules is determined by the number of all possible combinations of LTs of the input variables [27]). For example, when selecting three terms for each variable, the number of rules in the RB will be 81, which is already quite a large number, and can cause certain difficulties in its compilation. Therefore, in this case, it is proposed to organize the fuzzy DSS on the basis of a hierarchical principle, namely, to pre-group the second (flow speed V_F), third (particle concentration C_P) and fourth (particle sizes S_P) input variables into one additional variable "particle deposition rate" V_P by introducing an additional unit of fuzzy inference engine (FIE). In this case, it is advisable to separately group exactly these three variables, since together they can show how quickly the VEP will become clogged.

Thus, taking into account the foregoing, the structure of the proposed fuzzy DSS is shown in Figure 5.2, where INU and ONU are the input and output normalization units, which are used to convert input and output variables to relative units from their maximum values. The variables with asterisks ($D^\star_P$, $V^\star_F$, $C^\star_P$, $S^\star_P$, $I^\star_C$, $T^\star_C$, and $T^\star_R$) represent the corresponding variables in relative units and can vary in the range from 0 to 1.

The normalizing units are used to impart universal properties to the system. To do this, the input variables are divided by normalizing coefficients in the INU, and, in turn, the output variables are multiplied by the coefficients in the ONU. In this case, the values of these normalizing coefficients are equal

Figure 5.2: Functional structure of the fuzzy DSS for VEP maintenance planning.

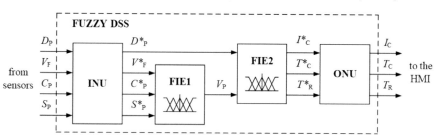

to the maximum values of the corresponding variables for specifically selected VEPs with certain performance and parameters. Thus, by introducing the necessary coefficient values, the system can be simultaneously used to plan the maintenance of various types of VEPs located in the enterprise, which differ significantly in performance.

In addition, the output variable I_C (cleaning intensity) can be designated as different intensities, depending on the type of VEP and the method of its cleaning. For example, for some VEPs, the intensity of air purge (flow rate of cleaning air) may be used when using this cleaning method.

Next, we will consider in detail directly the development of fuzzy logic inference units (FIE1 and FIE2) for this DSS. For both of these subsystems, the Mamdani type FIE is used, which includes stages of fuzzification, aggregation, activation, accumulation, and defuzzification [27, 28].

During the fuzzification stage, the current numerical values of input variables are translated into the corresponding sets of fuzzy terms, accompanied by the computation of membership degree values [27]. For the given input and output variables of the DSS, the following sets of linguistic terms are selected (Table 5.1).

The appearance of the linguistic terms for the input and output variables with the set parameters are shown in Figures 5.3 and 5.4, respectively.

The triangular and Gaussian (type 1) membership functions of LTs on the examples of variables I_C and D_P are represented by the expressions (5.3) and (5.4), respectively:

$$\mu(I_C) = \begin{cases} 0, & \text{at } I_C \leq a \text{ or } I_C \geq c; \\ \frac{I_C - a}{b - a}, & \text{at } a < I_C \leq b; \\ \frac{c - I_C}{c - b}, & \text{at } b < I_C < c; \end{cases} \tag{5.3}$$
$$a \leq b \leq c;$$

Table 5.1: Linguistic terms of the fuzzy DSS.

Variable	Number of LTs	Selected LTs	Type of membership function for LTs
D_P	5	Very low (VL); low (L); medium (M); High (H); very high (VH)	Gaussian, type 1
V_F	3	Low (L); medium (M); high (H)	Gaussian, type 1
C_P	3	Low (L); medium (M); high (H)	Gaussian, type 1
S_P	3	Small (S), medium (M), large (LG)	Gaussian, type 1
V_P	5	Very low (VL); low (L); medium (M); high (H); very high (VH)	Triangular
I_C	3	Low (L); medium (M); high (H)	Triangular
T_C	5	Very short (VSH); short (SH); medium (M); long (LN); very long (VLN)	Triangular
T_R	5	Very short (VSH); short (SH); medium (M); long (LN); very long (VLN)	Triangular

Figure 5.3: Appearance of the linguistic terms for the input variables.

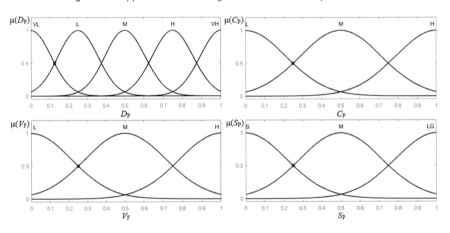

$$\mu(D_P) = e^{-\frac{(D_P - b)^2}{2a^2}}, \tag{5.4}$$

where a, b and c are the customizable parameters of the given membership functions.

Figure 5.4: Appearance of the linguistic terms for the output variables.

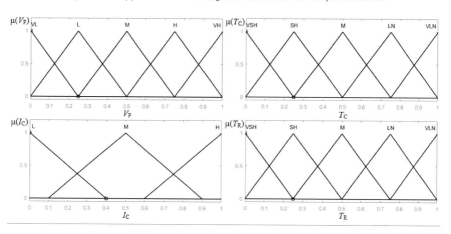

The rules within the RBs for the Mamdani-type subsystems FIE1 and FIE2 are articulated as follows:

$$\text{IF } ``V_F = A_{11}\text{'' AND ``}C_P = B_{11}\text{''AND ``}S_P = C_{11}\text{'' THEN ``}V_P = D_{11}\text{''}; \quad (5.5)$$

$$\begin{array}{c} \text{IF } ``D_P = A_{21}\text{'' AND ``}V_P = B_{21}\text{''} \\ \text{THEN } ``I_C = C_{21}\text{''AND ``}T_C = D_{21}\text{''AND ``}T_R = E_{21}\text{''}, \end{array} \quad (5.6)$$

where $A_{11}, B_{11}, C_{11}, D_{11}, A_{21}, B_{21}, C_{21}, D_{21}$, and E_{21} are certain linguistic terms of the corresponding variables. In this case, the rules for subsystem FIE1 are formed in the form of expression (5.5), and for subsystem FIE2 – based on expression (5.6).

In turn, the designed rule bases for the subsystems FIE1 and FIE2 are presented in Tables 5.2 and 5.3, respectively. In this case, the procedures of aggregation and activation are performed utilizing the "min" operation [27]. During the accumulation phase, the truncated membership functions identified in the preceding stage are amalgamated to derive the ultimate fuzzy subset of the output variable, employing the "max" operation. In addition, the defuzzification stage involves transitioning from the membership function of the output linguistic variable to its precise (numerical) value. For both of these subsystems, the numerical values of the output signals are determined using the center of gravity method [28].

The characteristic surfaces of the created fuzzy subsystems (FIE1, FIE2) are depicted in Figure 5.5. Specifically, the relationship $V_P = f(V_F, C_P)$ is established at $S_P = 0.5$.

Table 5.2: Rule base for the subsystem FIF1.

Rule number	LTs of input variables			LTs of output variable
	V_F	C_P	S_P	V_P
1	L	L	S	VL
2	L	L	M	VL
3	L	L	LG	VL
4	L	M	S	L
5	L	M	M	L
6	L	M	LG	M
7	L	H	S	M
8	L	H	M	M
9	L	H	LG	H
10	M	L	S	L
11	M	L	M	L
12	M	L	LG	M
13	M	M	S	M
14	M	M	M	M
15	M	M	LG	M
16	M	H	S	M
17	M	H	M	H
18	M	H	LG	H
19	H	L	S	M
20	H	L	M	M
21	H	L	LG	H
22	H	M	S	H

Table 5.2: Continued.

Rule number	LTs of input variables			LTs of output variable
	V_F	C_P	S_P	V_P
23	H	M	M	VH
24	H	M	LG	VH
25	H	H	S	VH
26	H	H	M	VH
27	H	H	LG	VH

Table 5.3: Rule base for the subsystem FIE2.

Rule number	LTs of input variables			LTs of output variables	
	D_P	V_P	I_C	T_C	T_R
1	VL	VL	L	VSH	VLN
2	VL	L	L	VSH	VLN
3	VL	M	L	VSH	VLN
4	VL	H	L	VSH	LN
5	VL	VH	L	SH	LN
6	L	VL	L	SH	LN
7	L	L	L	SH	LN
8	L	M	L	SH	LN
9	L	H	M	SH	M
10	L	VH	M	M	M
11	M	VL	L	M	M
12	M	L	M	M	M

Table 5.3: Continued.

Rule number	LTs of input variables			LTs of output variables	
	D_P	V_P	I_C	T_C	T_R
13	M	M	M	M	M
14	M	H	M	M	SH
15	M	VH	M	LN	SH
16	H	VL	M	LN	SH
17	H	L	H	LN	SH
18	H	M	H	LN	SH
19	H	H	H	LN	VSH
20	H	VH	H	VLN	VSH
21	VH	VL	H	VLN	VSH
22	VH	L	H	VLN	VSH
23	VH	M	H	VLN	VSH
24	VH	H	H	VLN	VSH
25	VH	VH	H	VLN	VSH

Hence, the intelligent decision support system created based on presented fuzzy subsystems FIE1 and FIE2 proves to be a valuable tool for generating essential recommendations to operators overseeing diverse types of vortex electrostatic precipitators across enterprises with varying profiles. As depicted in Figure 5.5, this system demonstrates efficient capability in producing the necessary parameters, including cleaning intensity, cleaning duration, and the remaining time until mandatory cleaning. These values are determined based on the real-time state of the VEP, showcasing the adaptability and effectiveness of the developed DSS for maintenance planning.

It should also be additionally noted that by using a hierarchical approach when creating a fuzzy DSS, it is possible to significantly reduce the total number of its rules. Namely, both sequentially connected fuzzy subsystems (FIE1 and FIE2) collectively have only 52 (27 + 25) rules, while one fuzzy subsystem with four inputs and a selected number of LTs would have 135 (5 × 3 × 3 × 3) rules

Figure 5.5: Characteristic surfaces of the created fuzzy subsystems FIE1, FIE2.

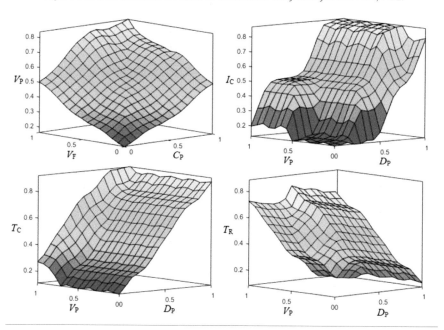

in the RB. This will substantially simplify the hardware and software part of the system during its further implementation.

5.4 Conclusions

This study has introduced an intelligent decision support system for the maintenance planning of vortex electrostatic precipitators, incorporating advanced technologies such as the Internet of Things and artificial intelligence. The primary objective of implementing this intelligent DSS is to minimize equipment downtime by optimizing cleaning modes and schedules. By leveraging real-time data and advanced algorithms, the system aims to enhance overall production efficiency across diverse enterprises. The integration of IoT and AI techniques not only ensures adaptive decision-making but also offers a comprehensive approach to maintenance planning, contributing to the sustained reliability and effectiveness of VEPs in various industrial settings.

Furthermore, the value of the intelligent DSS becomes evident in its ability to provide crucial recommendations for operators overseeing different types of vortex electrostatic precipitators within enterprises of varying profiles. The fuzzy subsystems FIE1 and FIE2 play a pivotal role in generating essential parameters such as cleaning intensity, cleaning duration, and the remaining time until mandatory cleaning. These recommendations are dynamically determined based on the real-time state of the VEP, showcasing the adaptability and efficiency of the developed DSS in maintenance planning. As industries continue to embrace advanced technologies, the presented intelligent DSS stands as a promising solution for optimizing VEP performance, reducing downtime, and ultimately contributing to the efficiency and sustainability of industrial processes. Moreover, a rather important point is that due to the use of a hierarchical approach when creating a DSS, the total number of rules in both fuzzy subsystems is 83 rules less than it would be in one subsystem built on the basis of the conventional approach, with four inputs and the same number of linguistic terms. In further research, it is planned to consider optimization of this DSS based on bio-inspired AI algorithms, as well as conduct a number of full-scale experiments.

Acknowledgments

This work was sponsored by the National Foreign Expert Program (Grant No. G2022014114L).

References

[1]   D. Renfrew, V. Vasilaki, E. Katsou, 'Indicator based multi-criteria decision support systems for wastewater treatment plants,' Science of The Total Environment, Vol. 915, 169903, 2024. https://doi.org/10.1016/j.scitoten v.2024.169903

[2]   Q. Ma, H. Li, 'A decision support system for supplier quality evaluation based on MCDM-aggregation and machine learning,' Expert Systems with Applications, Vol. 242, 122746, 2024. https://doi.org/10.1016/j.eswa.202 3.122746

[3]   H. Hu, et al., 'Development of the health decision support system (HDSS) in Canada and its implications in China,' 2016 12th International Conference on Natural Computation, Fuzzy Systems and Knowledge Discovery (ICNC-FSKD), Changsha, China, pp. 1391-1395, 2016. doi:10.1 109/FSKD.2016.7603381.

[4]   I. M., Jiskani, et al., 'An integrated fuzzy decision support system for analyzing challenges and pathways to promote green and climate smart

mining,' Expert Systems with Applications, Vol. 188, 116062, 2022. https://doi.org/10.1016/j.eswa.2021.116062

[5]   M. Solesvik, Y. Kondratenko, G. Kondratenko, I. Sidenko, V. Kharchenko, A. Boyarchuk, 'Fuzzy decision support systems in marine practice,' in: Fuzzy Systems (FUZZ-IEEE), 2017 IEEE International Conference on Fuzzy Systems, pp. 1-6, 2017. DOI:10.1109/FUZZ-IEEE.2017.8015471

[6]   L. Jiang, et al., 'A framework of emergency clinical decision support system based on MDA and resource model,' Proceedings of the 2014 IEEE 18th International Conference on Computer Supported Cooperative Work in Design (CSCWD), Hsinchu, Taiwan, pp. 451-456, 2014. doi:10.1109/CSCWD.2014.6846887.

[7]   Y. P. Kondratenko, S. B. Encheva, E. V. Sidenko, 'Synthesis of intelligent decision support systems for transport logistics,' in: Proceedings of the 6th IEEE International Conference on Intelligent Data Acquisition and Advanced Computing Systems, Prague, Czech Republic, pp. 642-646, 2011. DOI:10.1109/IDAACS.2011.6072847.

[8]   Y. Kondratenko, A. Shevchenko, Y. Zhukov, G. Kondratenko, O. Striuk, 'Tendencies and Challenges of Artificial Intelligence Development and Implementation,' in: Proceedings of the 12th IEEE International Conference on Intelligent Data Acquisition and Advanced Computing Systems: Technology and Applications, IDAACS'2023, Vol. 1, 2023, pp. 221-226, IDAACS 2023, Dortmund, Germany, 7-9 September 2023. DOI: 10.1109/IDAACS58523.2023.10348800

[9]   F. Camastra, et al., 'A Fuzzy Decision Support System for the Environmental Risk Assessment of Genetically Modified Organisms,' in: Bassis, S., Esposito, A., Morabito, F. (Eds.) Recent Advances of Neural Network Models and Applications. Smart Innovation, Systems and Technologies, vol 26. Springer, Cham, pp. 241-249, 2014. https://doi.org/10.1007/978-3-319-04129-2_24

[10]   E. B. Tirkolaee, N. S. Aydin, 'Integrated design of sustainable supply chain and transportation network using a fuzzy bi-level decision support system for perishable products,' Expert Systems with Applications, Vol. 195, 116628, 2022. https://doi.org/10.1016/j.eswa.2022.116628

[11]   O. Malanchuk, et al., 'A Neural Network Model-based Decision Support System for Time Management in Pediatric Diabetes Care Projects,' in: 2023 IEEE 18th International Conference on Computer Science and Information Technologies (CSIT), Lviv, Ukraine, pp. 1-4, 2023. doi:10.1109/CSIT61576.2023.10324014.

[12]   A. Rikalovic, et al., 'Intelligent Decision Support System for Industrial Site Classification: A GIS-Based Hierarchical Neuro-Fuzzy Approach,' in: IEEE Systems Journal, vol. 12, no. 3, pp. 2970-2981, 2018. doi:10.1109/JSYST.2017.2697043.

[13] S., Muthukaruppan, M. J. Er, 'A hybrid particle swarm optimization based fuzzy expert system for the diagnosis of coronary artery disease,' Expert Systems with Applications, 39(14), pp. 11657-11665, 2012. https://doi.org/10.1016/j.eswa.2012.04.036

[14] O.V. Kozlov, 'Optimal Selection of Membership Functions Types for Fuzzy Control and Decision Making Systems,' in: Proceedings of the 2nd International Workshop on Intelligent Information Technologies & Systems of Information Security with CEUR-WS, Khmelnytskyi, Ukraine, IntelITSIS 2021, CEUR-WS, Vol-2853, pp. 238-247, 2021. https://ceur-ws.org/Vol-2853/paper22.pdf

[15] Y. P. Kondratenko, A. V. Kozlov, 'Parametric optimization of fuzzy control systems based on hybrid particle swarm algorithms with elite strategy,' Journal of Automation and Information Sciences, Vol. 51, Issue 12, New York: Begel House Inc., pp. 25-45, 2019. DOI:10.1615/JAutomatInfScien.v51.i12.40

[16] P. Chatterjee, et al., 'IoT-based decision support system for intelligent healthcare – applied to cardiovascular diseases,' in: 2017 7th International Conference on Communication Systems and Network Technologies (CSNT), Nagpur, India, pp. 362-366, 2017. doi:10.1109/CSNT.2017.8418567.

[17] Y. Kondratenko, O. Gerasin, O. Kozlov, A. Topalov, B. Kilimanov, 'Inspection mobile robot's control system with remote IoT-based data transmission,' Journal of Mobile Multimedia. Special issue "Mobile Communication and Computing for Internet of Things and Industrial Automation", Vol. 17, Is. 4, pp. 499-522, 2021. DOI:https://doi.org/10.13052/jmm1550-4646.1742

[18] Y. P. Kondratenko, O. V. Korobko, O. V. Kozlov, 'Frequency Tuning Algorithm for Loudspeaker Driven Thermoacoustic Refrigerator Optimization,' Lecture Notes in Business Information Processing: Modeling and Simulation in Engineering, Economics and Management. – K. J. Engemann, A. M. Gil-Lafuente, J. M. Merigo (Eds.), Vol. 115, Berlin, Heidelberg: Springer-Verlag, pp. 270-279, 2012. https://doi.org/10.1007/978-3-642-30433-0_27

[19] V. M. Kuntsevich, V. F. Gubarev, Y. P. Kondratenko, D. V. Lebedev, V. P. Lysenko (Eds.), 'Control Systems: Theory and Applications', River Publishers, Gistrup, Delft, 2018. https://www.riverpublishers.com/book_details.php?book_id=668

[20] R. Duro, Y. Kondratenko (Eds.), 'Advances in intelligent robotics and collaborative automation,' River Publishers, Aalborg, 2015. doi:https://doi.org/10.13052/rp-9788793237049

[21] Y. Tian, et al., 'Development and experimental investigation of the narrow-gap coated electrostatic precipitator with a shield pre-charger

for indoor air cleaning,' Separation and Purification Technology, Vol. 309, 123114, 2023. https://doi.org/10.1016/j.seppur.2023.123114

[22] H. Shen, H. Jia, Y. Kang, 'Electrical Characteristics and Electrohydrodynamic Flows in Electrostatic Precipitator of Six Shaped Discharge Electrodes,' Journal of Applied Fluid Mechanics, Vol. 13, No. 6, pp. 1707-1718, 2020. DOI:10.36884/jafm.13.06.31085

[23] T. Song-Zhen, et al., 'Parametric optimization of H-type finned tube with longitudinal vortex generators by response surface model and genetic algorithm,' Applied Energy, Elsevier, vol. 239(C), pp. 908-918, 2019. DOI: 10.1016/j.apenergy.2019.01.122

[24] N. Grass, A. Zintl, E. Hoffmann, 'Enhanced Performance for Electrostatic Precipitators by Means of Conventional and Fuzzy Logic Control,' in: 2008 IEEE Industry Applications Society Annual Meeting, Edmonton, AB, Canada, pp. 1-4, 2008 doi:10.1109/08IAS.2008.100.

[25] R. M. Knight, et al. 'Development and optimisation of full-scale prototype electrostatic precipitators in a laboratory for particulate matter mitigation in poultryfacilities,' Biosystems Engineering, Vol. 230, pp. 71-82, 2023. https://doi.org/10.1016/j.biosystemseng.2023.03.019

[26] N. Grass, A. Zintl, E. Hoffmann, 'Electrostatic Precipitator Control Systems,' in: IEEE Industry Applications Magazine, vol. 16, no. 4, pp. 28-33, 2010, doi:10.1109/MIAS.2010.936967.

[27] O. Kozlov, G. Kondratenko, Z. Gomolka, Y. Kondratenko, 'Synthesis and Optimization of Green Fuzzy Controllers for the Reactors of the Specialized Pyrolysis Plants,' Kharchenko V., Kondratenko Y., Kacprzyk J. (eds) Green IT Engineering: Social, Business and Industrial Applications, Studies in Systems, Decision and Control, Vol 171, Springer, Cham, pp. 373-396, 2019. https://doi.org/10.1007/978-3-030-00253-4_16

[28] Y. P. Kondratenko, O. V. Kozlov, 'Mathematical Model of Ecopyrogenesis Reactor with Fuzzy Parametrical Identification,' Recent Developments and New Direction in Soft-Computing Foundations and Applications, Studies in Fuzziness and Soft Computing, Lotfi A. Zadeh et al. (Eds.), Berlin, Heidelberg: Springer-Verlag, Vol. 342, pp. 439-451, 2016. https://doi.org/10.1007/978-3-319-32229-2_30

Authors' Short CV

Lu Congxiang is an associate professor of the School of Intelligent Manufacturing at Yancheng Polytechnic College, who received a Ph.D. in Environmental Engineering from Jiangsu University in 2017. He has taken part in the implementation of the state project related to the optimization design of electrostatic precipitator since 2014. His main research directions include plasma desulfurization technology, optimization design of electrostatic precipitator, and computer aided design, etc.

Oleksiy Kozlov is a Doctor of Science in control processes automation, Professor of the Department of Intelligent Information Systems at Petro Mohyla Black Sea National University (PMBSNU), Ukraine. Since 2011 took part in the implementation of a number of international and state projects. His research interests include automation, intelligent information and control systems, fuzzy logic, bioinspired optimization techniques, and robotics.

Galyna Kondratenko is a Ph.D., Associate Professor, Associate Professor of the Intelligent Information Systems Department at Petro Mohyla Black Sea National University, Ukraine. She is a specialist in control systems, decision-making, fuzzy logic. She worked in the framework of international scientific university cooperation during the implementation of international projects with the European Union: TEMPUS (Cabriolet), Erasmus + (Aliot) and DAAD-Ostpartnerschaftsprogramm (project with the University of Saarland, Germany). Her research interests include computer control systems, fuzzy logic, decision-making, intelligent robotic devices.

Anna Aleksieieva is a Ph.D., Associate Professor, Associate Professor of the Ecology Department at Petro Mohyla Black Sea National University, Ukraine. She works in the framework of international scientific university cooperation in the implementation of UNIDO/GEF Project 'Global Cleantech Innovation Programme for Small and Medium Enterprises of Ukraine'. Her research interests include industrial ecology, radioecology, AI in environmental safety, energy transition, climate neutrality, green economy.

6

Leveraging Pre-trained Neural Networks for Image Classification in Audio Signal Analysis for Mobile Applications of Home Automation

V. I. Slyusar[1,*] and I. I. Sliusar[2]

[1]Institute of Artificial Intelligence Problems of MES and NAS of Ukraine, Kyiv, Ukraine
[2]Department of information systems and technologies, Poltava State Agrarian University Poltava, Ukraine
[*]Corresponding Author
Email: swadim@ukr.net, islyusar2007@ukr.net

Abstract

This chapter presents an in-depth analysis of innovative approaches in the field of audio signal classification using convolutional neural networks (CNNs) and their integration with image processing techniques. We investigate the effectiveness of transfer learning from image to audio domains, examining various neural network architectures like VGG16, DenseNet201, MobileNetV3Small, and EfficencyNet. Special emphasis is placed on the adaptability of these networks to handle audio data, particularly through the manipulation of input sizes and structures, such as Mel-frequency cepstral coefficients (MFCCs) and short-time Fourier transform (STFT) spectrograms.

Significant findings include the discovery that pre-trained image classification networks can be effectively repurposed for audio signal analysis. By adjusting parameters such as learning rate and batch size, and experimenting with different architectures, we achieved considerable improvements in classification accuracy. For instance, replacing MobileNet with a pre-trained EfficencyNet in a specific architecture resulted in a record accuracy of 82% at the 134th epoch.

Additionally, we explore the potential of these architectures for the unified processing of audio and image data, suggesting a method for task-specific commutation of input signals and weight loading in non-pre-trained layers. This approach highlights the versatility and potential of neural networks in handling diverse data types beyond their initial training scope.

Keywords: Convolutional neural network, architecture, audio signal, transformer, classification.

6.1 Introduction

In the rapidly evolving world of artificial intelligence (AI), numerous research and development efforts are continually redefining the boundaries of what is technically feasible and commercially viable. The realm of AI, with its interdisciplinary connections based on fields such as computer science, cognitive science, and engineering, has witnessed unprecedented growth, fostered by advancements in machine learning, neural networks, and big data analytics.

Current research in the field of AI is characterized by a combination of theoretical innovations and practical applications. Key areas such as deep learning, natural language processing (NLP), and robotics are rapidly evolving, leading to the emergence of new capabilities and applications. Concurrently, increasing attention is being paid to understanding and addressing the social and economic implications of AI, which is crucial for sustainable and responsible development. Looking towards the future, the prospective domains for AI implementation are diverse and multifaceted [1]. Sectors such as healthcare, automotive, finance, and education are poised for profound changes driven by AI integration. For instance, in healthcare, AI-based diagnostic tools [2, 3] and personalized treatment plans are revolutionizing patient care. In the automotive industry, autonomous vehicles and AI-enhanced manufacturing processes are changing the future of transportation. Similarly, in finance, AI is being employed for risk assessment, fraud detection, and algorithmic trading, transforming the landscape of financial services.

Exploring the latest advancements and predicting the potential applications of AI, researchers aspire to contribute to the ongoing discourse in the AI community and provide a foundation for future developments in this dynamic field. In this context, the current section is no exception. Following a broader discussion of the research trends and prospective domains of AI, it is essential to turn our attention to more specific applications that embody the forefront of AI technology. One such area is the use of pre-trained neural networks for image classification in the context of audio signal analysis, particularly in the realm of mobile applications for home automation. This chapter aims to analyze the intricacies of this application, underscoring its significance, challenges, and potential impact.

6.2 Use of Pre-trained Neural Networks for Image Classification

The advent of pre-trained neural networks has been a game-changer in the realm of image classification. These networks, trained on extensive datasets like ImageNet [4, 5], have exhibited remarkable abilities in identifying and classifying images with high accuracy. The deployment of such technology in mobile devices has opened up new avenues for real-time image analysis, which is particularly relevant in the context of smart home systems. In-home automation, image classification can be utilized for various purposes such as security (identifying individuals via surveillance cameras), appliance control (recognizing user gestures or actions), and even energy management (monitoring room occupancy and usage patterns).

The next important aspect is the search for desired photographs in extensive archives of snapshots created by anyone using smartphones, tablets, or digital cameras. The availability and simplicity of photo and video shooting processes, along with the constant increase in the storage capacities of these gadgets, have led to an exponential growth in the size of personal image and video databases. Consequently, finding a specific snapshot can become a time-consuming process, despite the efforts of software developers, such as Apple, who have been trying to address this issue for years. However, multilingual photo search, and even more so the search for specific scenes in video archives, has not yet achieved the necessary level of quality.

Another challenge lies in the need to optimize pre-trained neural network models for mobile platforms, where computational resources are more limited compared to traditional computing environments. This problem is further exacerbated by the increased image file sizes, which, along with the growing demands on hardware resources, largely negate the achievements of previous years. The voluminous datasets and corresponding neural networks created several years ago were oriented toward images with lower resolution.

6.3 Audio Signal Analysis in Home Automation. Combining Image and Audio Analysis for Comprehensive Home Automation

In parallel with image classification, audio signal analysis plays a key role in expanding the capabilities of home automation systems. The integration of artificial intelligence in processing and interpreting audio inputs provides a more intuitive and interactive user interface. Voice commands, ambient sound analysis, and acoustic monitoring can all become part of a sophisticated home automation ecosystem, making everyday tasks more convenient and efficient.

The complexity here lies not only in accurately recognizing voice commands in various accents and languages but also in distinguishing relevant sounds from background noise and interpreting non-verbal audio cues. Such challenges necessitate the development of advanced neural network architectures capable of handling the nuances of audio data.

In this context, a relevant task is the combination of image and audio analysis for comprehensive home automation, which opens up new possibilities.

Merging the capabilities of image classification and audio signal analysis heralds a new perspective in home automation. This synergy enables a more comprehensive understanding of the environment and user needs. For instance, a combined system can interpret both visual and auditory signals to more accurately determine the context of a command or more effectively identify security threats.

The integration of image classification and audio signal analysis capabilities on a single hardware platform allows for the unification of their processing through neural networks and simplifies the hardware requirements for their implementation. An important publication on this topic is a preprint [6], which proposed generalizing the well-established CLIP technology for joint processing of images, texts, and audio.

However, integrating all these domains into a mobile application for home automation is not without its challenges. It requires meticulous design to ensure uninterrupted operation, efficient use of computational resources, and strict data privacy measures. Moreover, the system must be adaptable and scalable to meet the evolving needs and preferences of users.

A more straightforward niche is the use of neural networks pre-trained on ImageNet for solving audio signal classification tasks. Overall, this idea is not new. A review of known solutions of this kind has been considered, for instance, concerning transformers in [7]. Specifically, in [8], a CNN-based image classification neural network was applied for music genre identification. The CNN model underwent preliminary training on the ILSVRC-2012 dataset, containing over 1 million natural images for classification, and was then utilized for genre classification using spectrogram images. For additional training, the GTZAN dataset [9, 10] was used.

In [11], the authors demonstrated that standard CNN models pre-trained on ImageNet can be effectively used as base networks for audio classification. Despite the significant difference between audio spectrograms and standard ImageNet image samples, the assumption of the validity of transfer learning was fully justified. Moreover, using weights pre-trained on ImageNet showed better results than using randomly initialized weights.

In the paper [12], the authors proposed the ESResNet model for the classification of environmental sounds, combining approaches in the fields of images and audio. The model is based on simple logarithmic spectrograms of short-term Fourier transform (STFT), processed using well-known approaches in the field of images. The use of attention blocks allowed the model to better focus on important information in the temporal and frequency domains of the input signal. This mechanism helped achieve high accuracy on standard datasets, making the model competitive compared to previous approaches.

The effectiveness of transfer learning from images to audio was also demonstrated by the authors of [13]. In this article, the feasibility of detecting anomalies in factory equipment operation through Mel-spectrograms of acoustic signals, characteristic of mechanical faults, is explored using neural networks pre-trained on image classification tasks. A similar approach was employed in [14] for the classification of siren signals from emergency service vehicles, such as fire engines and ambulances. In their work, the authors of [14] managed to achieve a siren signal recognition time of 0.0004 $\pm$ 5% seconds, a feat unattainable by any known large language model (LLM). This breakthrough challenges the prevailing misconception about the obsolescence of CNNs in current conditions, a misconception fueled by the boom in LLM development.

The further development of the idea of unifying neural networks for image and audio signal classification led to its generalization for transformer architectures [7]. As noted in [7, 15], transformers require more data for training compared to CNNs. Specifically, according to [15], to reliably surpass typical

CNNs in classification accuracy, a transformer needs to be trained on datasets exceeding 14 million images. This poses a challenge for using transformers in audio data analysis tasks, as typical audio signal datasets usually do not contain such large volumes of data. For this reason, transferring the learning results of transformers from the image domain to audio remains the preferred choice. Following this idea, the authors of [7] limited themselves to classifying audio spectrograms by adapting a ready-made vision transformer (ViT) that was pre-trained on a large array of images.

Concluding this brief overview of known solutions, it's important to note that a limitation of the discussed publications is their use of only spectrogram images (STFT or MFCC) for audio signal classification. In contrast, the study [16] proposed neural networks that enable joint processing of both types of spectrograms, as well as raw data (RAW). However, these networks did not use models pre-trained on the ImageNet dataset. In this context, it is suggested to bridge this gap by applying the concept to the task of music genre classification using the previously mentioned GTZAN dataset.

6.4 Experimentation Results with Different CNN Architectures

This section aims to examine the testing results of various convolutional neural network architectures for classifying 10 musical genres based on audio recordings: blues, jazz, disco, classical, pop, country, metal, rock, hip-hop, and reggae. The training dataset was obtained within the previously mentioned GTZAN [10] and contained 80 records for each class; the duration of each record was 30 seconds. The validation set consisted of 15 recordings per class.

As a starting point in the research, two convolutional architectures – a small and a large CNN (Figures 6.1 and 6.2, respectively) – were used. Their two branches were similar to the structures of neural networks for image classification and, in this case, were intended for separate processing of STFT and MFCC spectrograms. The third branch facilitated the processing of raw data sequences from the audio signal.

For forming the training batch, the batch size was set to 128. The Adam optimizer was configured with parameters Beta1 = 0.9, Beta 2 = 0.999, Epsilon = 10^{-7}, with the Amsgrad parameter disabled. The learning rate was set at 0.0001.

Under these conditions, the architecture in Figure 6.1 achieved an accuracy of 37.3% at the 20th epoch, followed by an overfitting effect. Further studies were conducted with a batch size 32. The less complex neural network, after

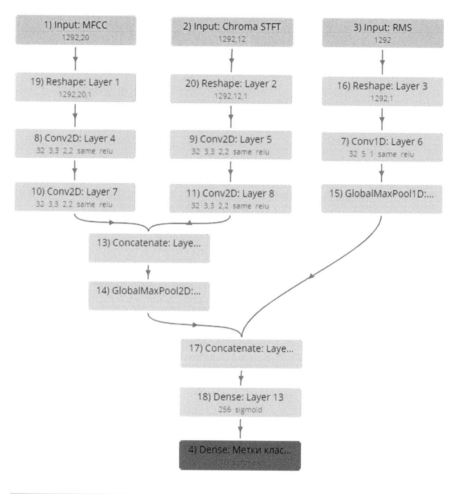

Figure 6.1: The small version of CNN architecture.

replacing the sigmoid in the output layer with ReLU and a batch size of 32, demonstrated an accuracy of 50.7%. For the larger neural network, after adjusting the parameters of the last dense layers, reducing their dimensionality from 512 to 200 and 80 respectively, and concurrently replacing the sigmoid with ReLU, an accuracy of 64% was achieved. The lowest classification accuracy was for the genre "blues" (20%), and the highest was for classical music.

Thus, in the considered case, batch size has a noticeable impact on classification accuracy. To confirm this, additional studies were conducted for

Figure 6.2: The big version of CNN architecture.

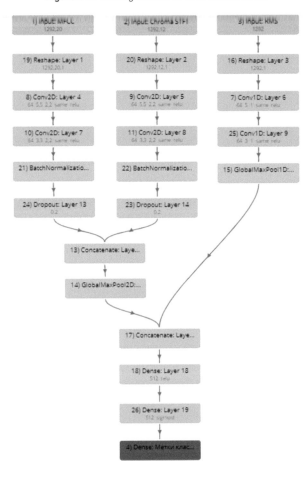

batches of 8, 16, and 64. Testing of the corresponding neural structures was carried out in the "Terra AI" framework [17].

In further studies, architectures with integrated image classification neural networks, pre-trained on the ImageNet dataset, were examined (Figure 6.2).

The first attempt of this kind was the integration of a pre-trained VGG16 into a standard neural network for processing audio signals (Figure 6.3). To better adapt VGG16 for audio content, a dense layer was added after it, reducing the number of outputs from 512 to 120.

Figure 6.3: Neural network for audio classification with pre-trained VGG16 CNN.

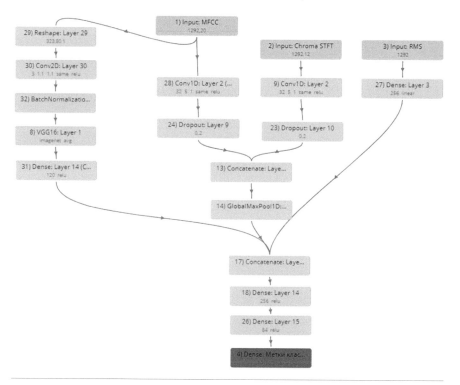

Adding VGG16 to the composition of a small three-input neural network was done in an additional branch of the architecture, while in the other three branches, typical processing of audio signals using one-dimensional convolutions (Conv1D) was maintained. The insertion of a normalizer at the VGG16 input led to a reduction of the learning rate to 0.0001, as the neural network simply did not train at rates of 0.01 and 0.001. As a result, accuracy increased to 56.7%, which had not been observed before for such an architecture in the considered experiment.

The further reduction to a learning rate of 0.00001 allowed increasing the average accuracy to 58.7% and further raising it to a record 62% (at the 130th epoch). The worst class accuracy rose to 33.3%. The obtained result confirmed the potential of using neural networks pre-trained on ImageNet for MFCC recognition.

Integrating a pre-trained DenseNet201 (Figure 6.4) instead of VGG16 into this architecture allowed achieving an accuracy BallancedRecall of 57.3% with

Figure 6.4: Neural network for audio classification with pre-trained DenseNet201 CNN.

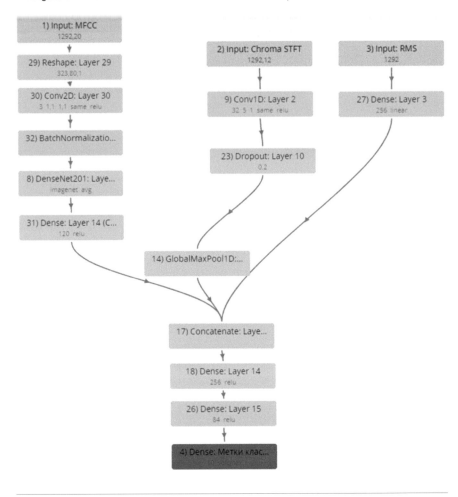

a variable training strategy and 60% with a fixed one at a learning rate of 0.0001 up to the 80th epoch, and then with 0.00001. A tensor of 323 × 80 × 3 is input into DenseNet201. This unconventional structure is permissible due to DenseNet201's adaptive input. From its output, a vector of 1920 elements is taken.

The accuracy matrix for DenseNet201 indicates the possibility of achieving more than 40% accuracy in two classes on the given dataset, which in the case of VGG16 had an accuracy of 33.3%. This suggests that it might be worthwhile to search for more successful architectures, as the dataset itself is not the reason for limitations in accuracy, at least not at the level of 33.3%.

Further improvement of the architecture was made by replacing Conv2D at the input of the normalizer in the branch with DenseNet201 with Conv2DTranspose. This led to a jump in accuracy to 64.7% at the 20th epoch with a learning rate of 0.0001. The subsequent switch at the 45th epoch to a rate of 0.00001 allowed for an increase in this figure to 67.3% at the 69th epoch. In this implementation, the lower threshold of accuracy for the worst-performing class rose from 33.3% to 40%. During the training process, classes migrate along the accuracy scale, with early epoch leaders being replaced by outsiders, dropping to lower levels, while classes initially positioned in the lower accuracy tier gradually move into the category of more accurate ones. There are also those whose accuracy remains frozen at one level and does not change with an increase in the number of training epochs at a fixed step. Overall, a more branched structure with a parallel convolutional branch tends to be somewhat more accurate.

It should be noted that the average class accuracy indicator does not always reflect the best set of weights for the neural network. Therefore, using as an indicator of training quality the mean value obtained by dividing the sum of the upper and lower accuracy range limits by 2 is proposed. This mean-calculated, centered accuracy profile tracks the maximum rise in accuracy of the worst-performing class, whereas traditional average class accuracy highlights cases where the maximum possible number of classes have as high accuracy as possible with an arbitrary lower bound.

The alternative architecture included, in addition to DenseNet201 in the MFCC evaluation branch, a pre-trained VGG16 in the STFT evaluation channel. At a learning rate of 0.001, an accuracy of 61.3% was achieved at the 27th epoch. With an initial and constant step of 0.0001, the accuracy was 64% at the 24th epoch and 66.7% at the 101st.

The next architecture included MobileNetV3Small and a dense element with increased outputs from 120 to 256 – in the MFCC channel. Additionally, in this same channel, a parallel simplified branch featured a reduction in the dropout rate to 0.1 and a replacement of GlobalMaxPooling with average GlobalMaxpooling2D. A similar replacement with AverageGlobalMaxpooling2D was also made in the STFT channel, which contained the same VGG16 with double expansion of the input image using Conv2DTranspose. All these changes led to a decrease in the learning rate. Initially, over 60 epochs, there were two to three classes for which classification did not begin at all, and the rock class had zero accuracy outliers up until the 124th epoch. At the same time, a group of six classes emerged with very high accuracy. Training started with a step of 0.0001. Then, at the 20th epoch, the step was reduced tenfold. As a result, an average accuracy of 66% was achieved at the 216th epoch, 67.3% at the 227th, and 68% at the 282nd epoch.

A more successful architecture was based on MobileNetV3Small with an input image format of 646 × 160 × 3 pixels for this pre-trained neural network (Figure 6.5). This audio sketch size was achieved using a Conv2DTranspose layer, configured with a 2 × 2 kernel and a 2 × 2 stride, effectively doubling the image dimensions. Similar settings were used for the same layer in the VGG16 channel. Additionally, the dense layers after the pre-trained MobileNetV3Small and VGG16 neural networks were eliminated in the MFCC and STFT channels. The maximum achieved accuracy was 68.7%.

An alternative variant was also explored, where before MobileNetV3, the image was increased not proportionally, but with a 2 × 3 coefficient, and in the VGG16 channel – 3 × 4. At the 270th epoch, this variant achieved an accuracy of 75.3%.

It should be noted that further preliminary enlargement of the original audio sketch dimensions with scaling factors of 3 × 4 in both channels of the same pre-trained neural networks did not lead to a proportional increase in accuracy. For example, an accuracy of 70.7% was achieved at the 163rd epoch and 73.3% at the 248th epoch. This indicates the presence of a certain optimal value of scaling factors, beyond which there is no increase in accuracy. One of the reasons for this phenomenon was a decrease in the upper limit of the accuracy range from 100% to 93.3%.

On the other hand, it is possible that for scaling up the audio sketch, more sophisticated procedures than those provided in Conv2DTranspose might be necessary.

To reduce the level of computational power requirements, an option was also considered for the preliminary combination of MFCC and STFT into a single frame, replacing two-channel processing with single-channel processing on one pre-trained neural network (Figure 6.6). A similar combination with RMS seems impractical, as the proportion of information in such a combined frame would be insignificant and the corresponding features could be ignored by the neural network.

Research on the structure in Figure 6.6 was conducted based on DenseNet121. At the 28th epoch, an accuracy of 64.7% was achieved with a learning rate of 0.0001.

Figure 6.5: The CNN architecture with MobileNetV3Small and VGG16.

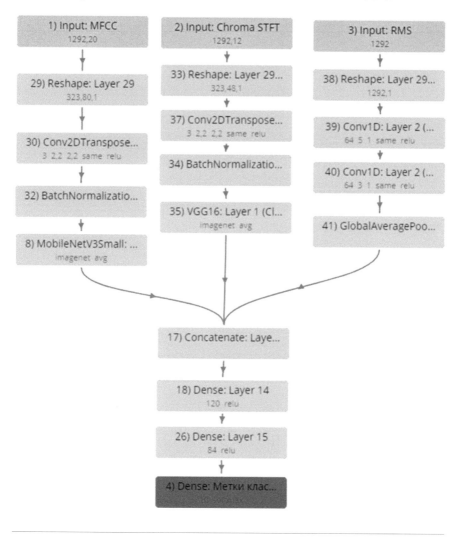

To increase the weight of STFT in the overall result, it's necessary to enlarge the dimensionality of the corresponding data tensor before merging with the MFCC channel, for instance, by using a Conv2DTranspose layer. Additionally, the use of a non-square expanding convolution deserves attention to avoid exceeding the power of available computational resources, while maximally approximating the format of the audio sketch at the input of the pre-trained network to a square shape.

Figure 6.6: CNN structure with a combination of MFCC and STFT into a single frame.

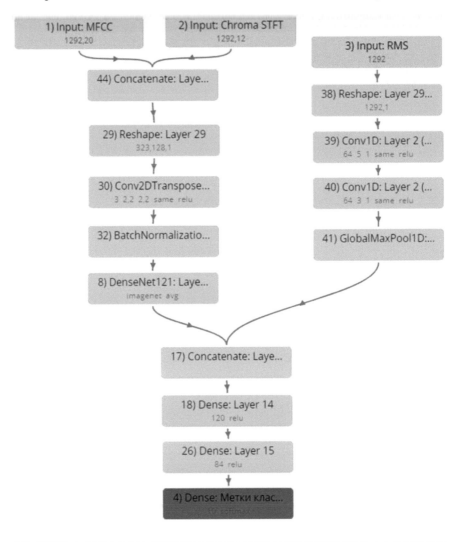

Similar research was conducted for the case of including VGG16 in the described variant. The result, however, turned out to be relatively ordinary. Overall, within the analyzed architectures, the two-channel scheme on average fell behind the three-channel solutions by several percent in average class accuracy. In this context, a promising approach could be the one that involves gradually discontinuing training for those classes that are already recognized with high accuracy, followed by focusing the neural network training only on those classes of audio data that are classified with high error. However, the methodology of such adaptive training requires further study.

In the final stage of the research, attention was focused on the multi-input implementation of the neural network, as presented in Figure 6.7.

Figure 6.7: The multi-input structure of the neural network.

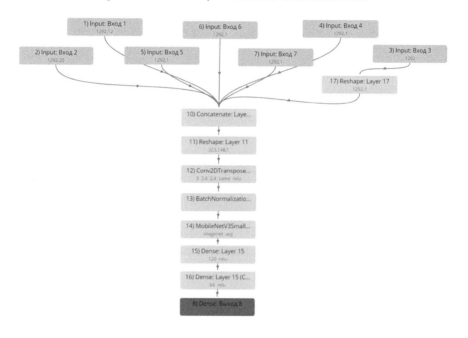

In addition to the previously used input data representations of MFCC (Mel-frequency cepstral coefficients), STFT (short-time Fourier transform), and RMS (root mean square), in this case, signal forms were used as additional input arrays in the form of:

(1) Audio signal, which is the basic form of sound information, and is typically represented as a wave or amplitude over time.

(2) Zero-Crossing rate (ZCR). This is a measure of the number of times in a given time frame that the amplitude of the audio signal passes through a value of zero. It's an indicator of the frequency content of the signal; a high ZCR can indicate a noisier and more high-frequency signal, while a low ZCR often corresponds to a more tonal signal.

(3) Spectral centroid. The spectral centroid is a measure used in digital signal processing to characterize a spectrum. It is indicative of the "center of mass" of the spectrum and is commonly

associated with the perceived brightness of a sound. It is calculated as the weighted mean of the frequencies present in the signal, determined using a Fourier transform, with their magnitudes as the weights.

(4) Spectral roll-off. This is the frequency below which a certain percentage (commonly 85% to 95%) of the total spectral energy of the signal is contained. It is used to distinguish between harmonic (voice) and noise-like (unvoiced) speech components.

(5) Spectral bandwidth. This refers to the width of a band of frequencies in a signal, generally centered around a central or dominant frequency. It's often used to describe the range of frequencies that a signal occupies. The spectral bandwidth gives an idea of how spread out the frequencies in your signal are around the spectral centroid.

Replacing the MobileNetV3Small neural network in the architecture shown in Figure 6.7 with a pre-trained EfficientNetB0 allowed achieving a record accuracy of 82% at the 134th epoch.

In addition to high accuracy in audio signal classification, the neural network variant shown in Figure 6.7 can serve as a basis for the unification of audio data and image processing. To achieve this, depending on the type of task being solved, it is necessary to implement appropriate commutation of input signals, and also load the necessary sets of weight coefficients for the specific case into those layers that are located outside the pre-trained neural network.

6.5 Conclusion

The research demonstrates that the utilization of neural networks, especially those pre-trained on image datasets like ImageNet, can be remarkably effective for audio signal classification tasks. The study shows that using neural networks, especially those pre-trained on image datasets such as ImageNet, can be extremely effective for audio classification tasks. In particular, the use of the EfficientNetB0 neural network pre-trained on images made it possible to achieve an average class accuracy of 82% when classifying 10 genres of music. At the same time, the three best results for genre recognition were received by classical (100%), metal (96.7%), jazz (90%). The outsiders were exactly disco (70%), country (73.3%) and rock (the same 73.3%). If we use the proposed indicator of the centered profile of the precision tube, the result will be better: $(100\%+70\%)/2 = 85\%$. The adaptability of such models, along with the implementation of architectural modifications and parameter optimizations, opens new frontiers in audio analysis. Our results suggest a promising direction for future research in the integration and unification of audio and visual data processing, potentially leading to more sophisticated and versatile AI systems. The versatility of these methods underscores the transformative potential of neural networks in various domains of data analysis and their significant role in advancing AI capabilities.

References

[1] Y. Kondratenko, A. Shevchenko, Y. Zhukov, G. Kondratenko, O. Striuk, 'Tendencies and Challenges of Artificial Intelligence Development and Implementation', Proceedings of the 12th IEEE International Conference on Intelligent Data Acquisition and Advanced Computing Systems: Technology and Applications, IDAACS'2023, Vol. 1, 2023, pp. 221 – 226, IDAACS 2023, Dortmund, Germany, 7-9 September 2023.

[2] A. Sheremet, Y. Kondratenko, I. Sidenko, G. Kondratenko, 'Diagnosis of Lung Disease Based on Medical Images Using Artificial Neural Networks', 2021 IEEE 3rd Ukraine Conference on Electrical and Computer Engineering, UKRCON 2021 - Proceedings, pp. 561–566, 2021.

[3] Y. Kondratenko, I. Sidenko, G. Kondratenko, V. Petrovych, M. Taranov, I. Sova, 'Artificial Neural Networks for Recognition of Brain Tumors on MRI Images', in: A. Bollin, et al. (eds), Information and Communication Technologies in Education, Research, and Industrial Applications. ICTERI 2020. Communications in Computer and Information Science, vol. 1308, Springer, Cham, pp. 119-140, 2021. DOI:https://doi.org/10.1007/978-3-030-77592-6_6

[4] J. Deng, W. Dong, R. Socher, et al., 'Imagenet: A large-scale hierarchical image database', 2009 IEEE conference on computer vision and pattern recognition, IEEE, pp. 248-255, 20 June 2009, DOI:10.1109/CVPR.2009.5206848.

[5] V. Slyusar, et al., 'Improvement of the object recognition model on aerophotos using deep convolutional neural network', Eastern-European Journal of Enterprise Technologies, vol. 5, No. 2(113), pp. 6–21, 2021, DOI:10.15587/1729-4061.2021.243094.

[6] A. Guzhov, F. Raue, J. Hees, A. Dengel, 'AudioCLIP: Extending CLIP to Image, Text and Audio', 24 June 2021, https://arxiv.org/abs/2106.13043v1.

[7] Y. Gong, Y.-A. Chung, J. Glass, 'AST: Audio Spectrogram Transformer', 8 July 2021, https://arxiv.org/pdf/2104.01778.pdf.

[8] G. Gwardys, D. M. Grzywczak, 'Deep image features in music information retrieval', IJET, vol. 60, no. 4, pp. 321–326, 2014, DOI:10.2478/eletel-2014-0042.

[9] G. Tzanetakis, P. Cook, 'Musical genre classification of audio signals', IEEE Transactions on Audio and Speech Processing, vol. 10(5), pp. 293–302, 2002, DOI:10.1109/TSA.2002.800560.

[10] 'GTZAN Dataset - Music Genre Classification', URL:https://www.kaggle.com/datasets/andradaolteanu/gtzan-dataset-music-genre-classification.

[11] K. Palanisamy, D. Singhania, A. Yao, 'Rethinking CNN models for audio classification', 2020, https://arxiv.org/abs/2007.11154.

[12]   A. Guzhov, F. Raue, J. Hees, A. Dengel, 'ESResNet: Environmental sound classification based on visual domain models', ICPR, pp. 4933-4940, 2021, DOI:10.1109/ICPR48806.2021.9413035.

[13]   R. Muller, F. Ritz, S. Illium, C. Linnhoff-Popien, 'Acoustic anomaly detection for machine sounds based on image transfer learning', 2020, URL:https://arxiv.org/pdf/2006.03429.pdf.

[14]   A. A. Lisov, A. Z. Kulganatov, S. A. Panishev, 'Using convolutional neural networks for acoustic based emergency vehicle detection', Modern Transportation Systems and Technologies, vol. 9(1), pp. 95-107, 2023, DOI:10.17816/transsyst20239195-107

[15]   A. Dosovitskiy, L. Beyer, A. Kolesnikov, D. Weissenborn, X. Zhai, T. Unterthiner, M. Dehghani, M. Minderer, G. Heigold, S. Gelly, J. Uszkoreit, N. Houlsby, 'An image is worth 16x16 words: Transformers for image recognition at scale', ICLR, 2021, https://arxiv.org/abs/2010.11929

[16]   V.-T. Tran, W.-H. Tsai, 'Acoustic-Based Emergency Vehicle Detection Using Convolutional Neural Networks', IEEE Access, Volume 8, 2020, 10.1109/ACCESS.2020.2988986.

[17]   V. Slyusar, et al., 'Improving a neural network model for semantic segmentation of images of monitored objects in aerial photographs', Eastern-European Journal of Enterprise Technologies, vol. 6/2 (114), pp. 86–95, 2021, DOI:10.15587/1729-4061.2021.248390.

Authors' Short CV

Vadym Slyusar is a Doctor of Science, Professor, Honoured Scientist and Technician of Ukraine (2008). He received a Ph.D. in 1992, Doctor of Sciences in 2000, Professor in 2005. His research spans digital information processing, computational algorithms in various fields like radars, communications, and AI-based systems including deep machine learning and computer vision. He introduced innovative matrix operations widely used in machine learning and statistical data processing. His contributions have led to new research directions in data transmission and MIMO systems, as well as technological advancements in hardware and software, including augmented and mixed reality systems.

Ihor Sliusar is a Ph.D., Associate Professor. Associate Professor of the Department of Information Systems and Technologies Poltava State Agrarian University. He received a Ph.D. in 2004, Associate Professor in 2006. His research spans digital information processing, computational algorithms in various fields like communications, IoT and AI-based systems including deep machine learning and computer vision.

Effectiveness Evaluations of Optical Color Fuzzy Computing

Victor Timchenko[1], Vladik Kreinovich[2], Yuriy Kondratenko[3,4], and Volodymyr Horbov[1]

[1]Admiral Makarov National University of Shipbuilding, Ukraine
[2]University of Texas at El Paso
[3]Petro Mohyla Black Sea National University, Ukraine
[4]Institute of Artificial Intelligence Problems of MES and NAS of Ukraine
E-mail: vl.timchenko58@gmail.com, vladik@utep.edu,
y_kondrat2002@yahoo.com, volodymyr.horbov@gmail.com

Abstract

This chapter describes the special artificial intelligence technique for increasing efficiency of fuzzy information processing. The approach proposed by the authors consists of representing input fuzzy information as color information quanta with the ability to carry out logical operations with them based on the transformation of light radiation. It is shown that this approach provides obvious advantages of increasing the speed of logical calculations due to direct processing (without digitalization) of large fuzzy input data. The spaces of change in input fuzzy data during their binary processing have been studied and a comparative analysis with the architecture of optical computing has been carried out. A predictive assessment of the proposed designs of optical architecture elements (coloroids) in terms of energy consumption during the calculation process is given and a positive conclusion is made regarding the satisfaction of accepted requirements for energy efficiency. Directions for further development of optical color computing are also determined.

Keywords: Optical color computing, fuzzy data, logical coloroid, effectiveness.

7.1 Introduction

The undoubted growth of interest in optical computing, including that based on incredible achievements in the field of optical transmission of large volumes of information, is also due to the unprecedented intensity of the search for solutions in the field of artificial intelligence and the discovery of extensive opportunities for increasing processor performance. Constantly developing research on the creation of all-optical logic devices for binary and fuzzy calculations is given in [1–7] and is based on the use of the effects of holography and polarization of light, the use of diffraction and interference phenomena in circuits using prism matrices, as well as using other principles of optical physics. It should be noted that the technologically complex feasibility of the proposed devices currently seriously hinders their widespread use.

From the point of view of using light emitters in optical logic elements, work in quantum optics on the creation of energy-efficient designs of fiber lasers and laser LEDs with minimal pulse characteristics is also of great interest [8].

A wide analysis of the prospects and advantages of optical computing is carried out in the work [9]. The following properties of optical computing are analyzed in detail:

- almost dissipative dynamics;
- transmission with low energy losses;
- spatial parallelism;
- throughput;
- the ability to intersect light rays and their software control at high speed;
- robustness and others.

Undoubtedly, when creating optical logic elements, it is necessary, following the widely recognized and experimentally confirmed Landauer's principle [10–12], to evaluate the energy costs when performing computational operations. These works experimentally validated the requirement for ultra-low-power electronics architectures to satisfy the limit of Landauer's principle as evidence of their effectiveness. Energy efficiency is one of the most important principles for comparing the performance of optical and semiconductor computing elements.

In [13], the author conducts a detailed comparative analysis of electrical and optical computing from the point of view of energy costs. The conclusions of these studies for an optical computing system based, for example, on modulation of light waves and binary encoding of input signals, are that the energy costs of electrical and optical systems are approximately the same. The author assumes that the calculations are carried out with the same high accuracy and do not cover optical calculations with fuzzy input information and the use of neural networks. At the same time, [14], devoted to similar topics for computational neural networks, has shown significantly higher computational speeds and energy efficiency of all-optical computing systems.

Let's think about what underlies the initial thoughts of the human mind: words, numbers, images, or others. Let's imagine a person's reasoning when crossing the road: a pedestrian looks at the road, sees an approaching car and approximately determines the distance to it and his initial speed of crossing the road – this is proportional to the error of the component of the law on regulating the crossing. Knowing from experience that this is inaccurate, he approximately determines the speed of the approaching car, thereby carrying out the differentiation function, this is the differential component of the transition control law. An experienced pedestrian knows that he often makes mistakes when crossing (for example, due to poor vision), and by integrating his errors, he adds the resulting sum of errors to the same law of crossing control. That is, the human mind performs PID control functions, further adjusting its speed or acceleration in the process of moving through a transition depending on the changing situation.

This is great, but how does this happen and does it require a verbal or numerical estimate of the distance, the speed of the approaching vehicle, and the accumulated error? Yes, if you need to share this with your companion, otherwise it is more logical to assume that perhaps the assessment by the human senses is expressed in some degree of danger during the transition and this sensation directly enters the physiological organs of the person, for example, releasing a corresponding amount of adrenaline and accelerating desire to avoid danger. What degrees of danger could these be? It is logical to present them as follows: "extremely dangerous", "very dangerous", "dangerous", "rather not dangerous", "not dangerous", and "safe".

So, we have six degrees of danger. In the works of Zadeh and other authors, for example, [15–21], qualitative (fuzzy) information is described by linguistic variables (fuzzy sets). However, in this case, two problems arose, one arising from the other: it is impossible to directly carry out logical operations with linguistic variables, i.e. to handle linguistic variables one must first move to digital distributions. One of the new directions for using an alternative representation of a fuzzy set in the form of a light emitter of a certain color is presented in [22, 23].

Naturally, the development of computer systems now makes it possible to process data at speeds up to the reached technological ceiling of 10^{14} operations/s; however, if we do not need high accuracy of estimates concerning operations with fuzzy sets, including only six stages of distributions, then perhaps will there be a release of computing power that is spent on their binary processing, which will increase the speed of calculations with fuzzy data above 10^{14} operations/s?

7.2 Formulation of the Tasks

The first task that we intend to solve in this article is that it is necessary to determine whether it is possible to implement devices that, when assessing the type of linguistic variables or similar types of assessments, allow the logical operations of disjunction, conjunction, negation, idempotency to be performed with them, and others. The second challenge is to determine what we lose in computational performance and energy costs by using binary digital encoding versus processing fuzzy information as directly as possible.

7.3 Optical Color Fuzzy Computing

To solve the first problem, the authors in [24–27] proposed representing fuzzy information in the form of six specific colors. It is natural to represent the linguistic variables or fuzzy sets considered above for a six-step distribution with the following quanta of a certain color: "extremely dangerous" – red $\{R\}$, "very dangerous" – yellow $\{Yel\}$, "dangerous" – magenta $\{M\}$, "rather not dangerous" – green $\{G\}$, "not dangerous" – cyan $\{C\}$, "safe" – blue $\{B\}$. In this case, white light $\{W\}$ is associated as a "positive" and "new" solution, and black $\{Blc\}$ as an empty quantum, the "absence" of a solution.

We often encounter a similar distribution or parts of it in everyday life, for example, these are traffic lights and this is quite enough for us to regulate the movement of pedestrians and cars. You can also give examples of the degrees of radiation, fire and other types of hazards. These representations for a specific color are described in more detail in [24–27]. Thus, everything looks, in our opinion, very well-reasoned with the encoding of fuzzy information.

Further, [24] show a new, most important, in our opinion, property of the long-known colorimetric transformations of light – this is that the additive and subtractive transformation of light radiation of a certain color by light filters of a certain color are identical to disjunction, conjunction, negation, idempotence and other logical operations. Examples of such operations are shown by the following formulas, respectively for:

- Disjunction

$$\{R\}\lor\{G\}\lor\{B\} = \{W\};\ \{R\}\lor\{G\} = \{Yel\};\ \{R\}\lor\{B\} = \{M\};\ \{G\}\lor\{B\} = \{C\}$$

- Conjunction

$$\{W\} \land \{R\} \land \{G\} \land \{B\} = \{Blc\}$$

- Idempotence

$$\{R\} \lor \{R\} = \{R\};\ \{G\} \lor \{G\} = \{G\};\ \{B\} \lor \{B\} = \{B\}$$

- Negation

$$(\{R\} \lor \neg\{R\}) \land \{B\} = \{B\}.$$

Developing the proposed approach, the authors proposed and studied optical logic devices (coloroids) [26, 27] with 3, 6, 12, and also propose in this work a two-level coloroid with 45 channels for inputting fuzzy color information. An optical system with 45 fuzzy evaluations inputs **Q** based on four basic coloroids with 12 inputs is an example of the implementation of a primary coloroid information processing and inference network with more than six hundred possible variants of logical operations (Figure 7.1). In the case of an output estimate of $\{Blc\}$ (no light emitter), a new solution is generated in the form of white light emitter to the input of the coloroid system.

Examples of implementation of matrix logical operations for some combinations of input information (according to the combination of estimates, transformed by color filters, presented in Figure 7.1):

- I hieratical network:
- Coloroid Col_1^I, for input set $\{R,G,B\}$:

$$\{R\} \lor \{G\} \lor \{B\} = \{W\};$$

filters $\{Yel,C\}$

$$\{W\} \wedge \{B\} \wedge \{R\} = \{G\},$$

filters $\{M, C\}$

$$\{W\} \wedge \{G\} \wedge \{R\} = \{B\},$$

filters $\{M,Yel\}$

$$\{W\} \wedge \{G\} \wedge \{B\} = \{R\},$$

disjunction

$$\{R\} \vee \{G\} \vee \{B\} = \{W\};$$

filters $\{Yel,M,C\}$:

$$\{W\} \wedge \{B\} \wedge \{G\} \wedge \{R\} = \{Blc\}$$

- Coloroid Col_2^I, for input set $\{R,B,B\}$:

$$\{R\} \vee \{B\} \vee \{B\} = \{M\};$$

filters $\{Yel,C\}$

$$\{M\} \wedge \{B\} \wedge \{R\} = \{Blc\},$$

filters $\{M,C\}$

$$\{M\} \wedge \{G\} \wedge \{R\} = \{B\},$$

filters $\{Yel,M\}$

$$\{M\} \wedge \{B\} \wedge \{G\} = \{R\},$$

disjunction

$$\{Blc\} \vee \{B\} \vee \{R\} = \{M\};$$

filters $\{Yel,M,Yel\}$

$$\{M\} \wedge \{B\} \wedge \{G\} \wedge \{B\} = \{R\};$$

- Coloroid Col_3^I, for input set $\{G,B,B\}$:

$$\{G\} \vee \{B\} \vee \{B\} = \{C\};$$

filters $\{C,M\}$

$$\{C\} \wedge \{R\} \wedge \{G\} = \{B\},$$

filters $\{M,M\}$

$$\{C\} \wedge \{G\} \wedge \{G\} = \{B\},$$

filters $\{C,C\}$

$$\{C\} \wedge \{R\} \wedge \{R\} = \{B\},$$

Figure 7.1: An example of the implementation of logical operations for a two-level coloroid.

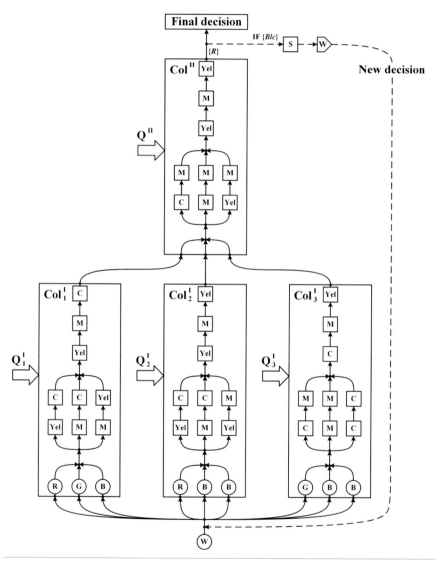

disjunction

$$\{B\} \vee \{B\} \vee \{B\} = \{B\};$$

filters $\{C,M,Yel\}$

$$\{B\} \wedge \{R\} \wedge \{G\} \wedge \{B\} = \{Blc\};$$

- II hieratical network, Col^{II} for input set $\{Blc,R,Blc\}$:

$$[Blc] \vee [R] \vee [Blc] = [R];$$

filters $\{C,M\}$

$$\{R\} \wedge \{R\} \wedge \{G\} = \{Blc\},$$

filters $\{M,M\}$

$$\{R\} \wedge \{G\} \wedge \{G\} = \{R\},$$

filters $\{Yel,M\}$

$$\{R\} \wedge \{B\} \wedge \{G\} = \{R\},$$

disjunction

$$\{Blc\} \vee \{R\} \vee \{R\} = \{R\};$$

filters $\{Yel,M,Yel\}$

$$\{R\} \wedge \{B\} \wedge \{G\} \wedge \{B\} = \{R\}, \textbf{\textit{final decision.}}$$

The developed designs of optical logic coloroids, when performing the basic logical operations of disjunction and conjunction, do not contain switching elements (unlike semiconductor ones) and are thus quite technologically advanced.

The given general principles for constructing optical logical coloroids require clarification of the designs of their individual elements, for example, those used in the coloroid, when generating the solution output and, if necessary (due to the lack of a primary solution), generating a new solution using a white light emitter WS. This will be a laser diode with a pulsed operating principle. Work in the field of quantum optics shows [8] that when a laser pulse is implemented, the pulse duration can reach femtoseconds (10^{-15} s).

7.4 Estimating Fuzzy Sets Operations

7.4.1 Explanation of fuzzy set operations on scalar machines

The code for a single-threaded implementation of the unification operation in C using the method of sequential calculation of scalar elements will take the following form:

```
for (uint8_t i=0; i<SIZE; i++){
        if (aR[i]>aB[i])
        RuB[i]=aR[i];
        else RuB[i]=aB[i];
}
```

The very essence of the unification operation lies in the lines:

```
if (aR[i]>aB[i])
RuB[i]=aR[i];
else RuB[i]=aB[i];
```

which must be repeated for each element of the fuzzy set. This is shown schematically in Figure 7.2.

Figure 7.2: Principle of unification operation on scalar machines.

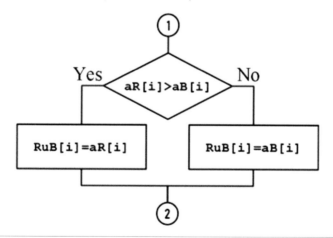

The intersection operation code and principle will be similar except for the line:

```
if (aR[i]<aB[i])
```

The assembly code consists of instructions for comparing array elements and assignment of a value to the resulting element. For each architecture, there will be a corresponding number of cycles required to execute the corresponding instruction.

Computing the operation of simultaneous unification of n fuzzy sets of m elements (Figure 7.3) on the processor with a single-threaded implementation in C language using the method of sequential calculation of scalar elements will take the number of cycles calculated by the formula:

$$(n - 1) \times m \times x,$$

where n – number of fuzzy sets; m – number of elements in fuzzy sets Q; x – number of cycles for performing the comparison of two elements and assigning the result.

Intersection can be done only sequentially (n is equal to 2), so the number of cycles for intersections of two fuzzy sets with m elements is calculated as follows:

$$m \times x.$$

Since each element of the fuzzy array is calculated independently of the other, this process can be parallelized. This can be done using a processor with a number of threads greater than or equal to the number of elements of sets.

Given

$$\text{Clock rate} = \frac{\text{Clock cycles}}{\text{Seconds}}.$$

The time for performing the unification or intersection operation of two elements from two fuzzy sets will be:

$$\text{Time} = \frac{\text{Clock cycles}}{\text{Clock rate}}.$$

However, a more efficient way may be to use a different approach, for example, FPGA [28, 29, 30]. In this way, it is possible to configure a logical block that will perform a comparison and assignment operation in one clock cycle of a synchronous pulse. It is worth considering that, unlike the clock rate of CPU, which can be measured in GHz (up to 6 GHz), a synchronous pulse is usually calculated in hundreds of MHz (100–500 MHz). The performance of the operation on FPGA can be calculated as follows:

$$Time \frac{1}{f_{clk}} + T_{delay},$$

$$T_{delay} = t_{setup} + t_{cq} + t_{logic},$$

where f_{clk} – synchronous pulse; t_{setup} – minimum time, the input signal must be stable before the clock edge for proper operation; t_{cq} – time, taken for the output to stabilize after the clock edge; t_{logic} – time, taken by the logic circuitry to produce a valid output.

7.4.2 Estimation of effectiveness of fuzzy set operations between architectures

The ARM architecture is designed for small-format and embedded solutions. The x86-x64 architecture is more complex, and bulky, but faster. FPGA has a low clock frequency but can create the simplest and most efficient electronic logic, which can serve as a prototype for creating ISICs.

For the Cortex M4 family of processors, the number of cycles (x) will be equal to 26 [31]. The maximum frequency of such processors is 240 MHz [32]. The unification operation with the number of fuzzy sets (n) equal 9 and the number of elements of fuzzy sets (m) equal 6 will take 1248 cycles when executed single-threaded according to the formula above and 234 cycles when computing each element in parallel (impossible on Cortex-M4, but possible on more expensive and advanced ARM architecture families). More advanced families like Cortex-A78, Cortex-A710, Cortex-A715, Cortex-A720 (frequency up to 3 GHz) can have up to 14 cores, Cortex-X1, Cortex-X2 (frequency up to 3 GHz), Cortex-X3 (3.25 GHz), Cortex-X4 (3.4 GHz) – up to 10 cores. They also have a 64-bit architecture, versus the 32-bit Cortex-M4.

Similarly, $\times 86-\times 64$ architecture processors supporting a standard instruction table [33] execute the code in 8 cycles $(x = 8)$. When calculating each element of a fuzzy set in parallel, it will take 72 cycles according to the formula above. Typically, frequencies of consumer desktop processors can reach 6 GHz and the number of cores greater than 6 is not uncommon.

Execution on FPGA does not require special comments. The code is executed in one clock cycle of the synchronous generator.

However, it is important to clarify that it is almost impossible to calculate the number of cycles required to execute a certain code on complex superscalar processors (this applies to both multi-core ARM and $\times 86-\times 64$ processors) and the given values are very relative. The number of cycles and the actual execution of instructions will vary from processor to processor and depend on such things as the design features of the processor (what operations it was made for) and on technologies that are used in modern superscalar processors such as out-of-order execution, branch prediction, and pipelining. In addition, in a real application, the execution efficiency, including for an FPGA, will also depend on its design and structure and the presence of communication through external memory communication interfaces. Actual performance may be affected by factors such as routing delays, specific technology characteristics, and the overall design of the FPGA chip. The formula provided above is a simplified representation and may require adjustments based on chip specifications and synthesis settings.

Without relying on specific code execution by concrete models and families of chips, average values for each architecture were calculated for operation of unification (disjunction) of n fuzzy sets and presented in Table 7.1 and Figure 7.4 (in normal (a) and logarithmic (b) forms), as well as for operation of intersections (conjunction) of n fuzzy sets shown in Table 7.2 and Figure 7.5 in normal (a) and logarithmic (b) forms.

Table 7.1: Number of cycles required to perform the operation of unification.

Sets	ARM (serial)	ARM	×86–×64	FPGA	Coloroid
2	156	26	8	1	1
3	312	52	16	2	1
4	468	78	24	3	1
5	624	104	32	4	1
6	780	130	40	5	1
7	936	156	48	6	1
8	1092	182	56	7	1
9	1248	208	64	8	1

Figure 7.3: Operation of unification (disjunction) of n fuzzy sets **Q**.

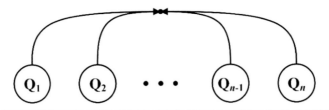

Additionally, since FPGA and coloroid are the same in the last comparison, a comparison of the number of logical blocks and filtering blocks of FPGA and coloroid is provided in Table 7.3 and Figure 7.7.

Figure 7.4: Comparison between different architectures performing the operation of unification: normal (a) and logarithmic (b).

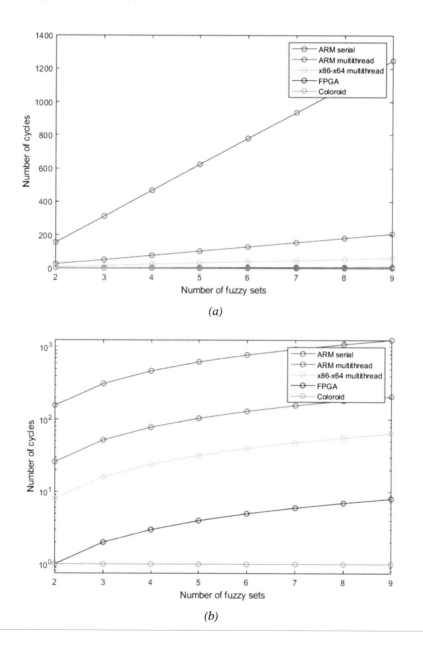

(a)

(b)

Table 7.2: Number of cycles required to perform the operation of intersection.

Sets	ARM (serial)	ARM	×86–×64	FPGA	Coloroid
2	156	26	8	1	1
3	312	52	16	2	2
4	468	78	24	3	3
5	624	104	32	4	4
6	780	130	40	5	5
7	936	156	48	6	6
8	1092	182	56	7	7
9	1248	208	64	8	8

Figure 7.5: Operation of intersections (conjunction) of n fuzzy sets **Q** sequentially.

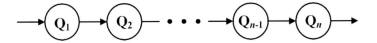

Table 7.3: Number of blocks required to perform the operation of intersection.

	Blocks							
Sets	2	3	4	5	6	7	8	9
Coloroid	1	2	3	4	5	6	7	8
FPGA	6	12	18	24	30	36	42	48

7.5 Energy Analysis

Energy analysis of optical computing operations needs to be carried out for a comparative assessment of optical and semiconductor devices, although this will be quite approximate given the current impossibility of accurately estimating the nanoscale dimensions of optical coloroids. We use the limitation

Figure 7.6: Comparison between different architectures performing the operation of intersection: normal (a) and logarithmic (b).

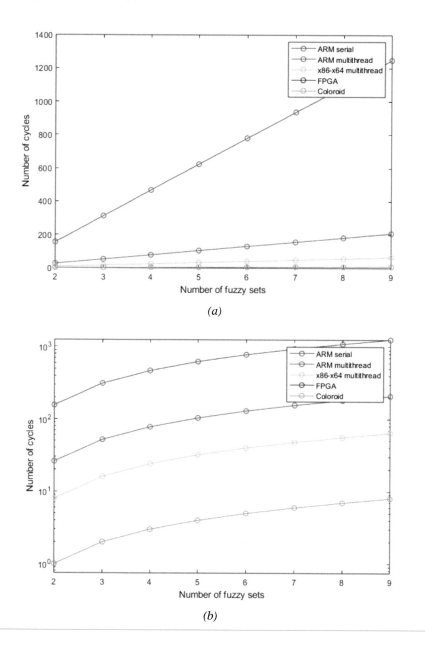

(a)

(b)

Figure 7.7: Comparison between FPGA and coloroid in the number of blocks required to perform the operation of intersection

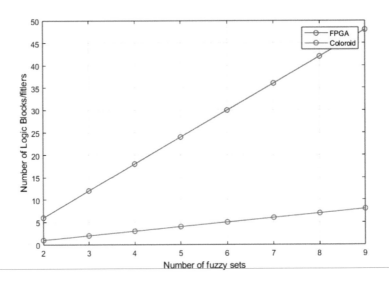

established by Landauer's principle on the minimum energy consumption when processing one bit of information [10], according to the formula $E_{min} \geq kT \ln 2$, where k is Boltzmann's constant and T is absolute temperature, and is 2.8×10^{-21} J.

Considering the computing architecture of the given coloroid network based on calculations of binary calculations when processing fuzzy sets, we can suggest that the number of binary operations will be about $N \approx 10^3$ operations.

With an allowable laser emitter power of $P = 1$ mW and a radiation pulse duration of $\tau = 5$ fs (10^{-15} s), we obtain the energy E_l expended for one equivalent binary operation

$$E_l = \frac{P \times \tau}{N} = 5 \times 10^{-3} \times 10^{-15} \times 10^{-3} = 5 \times 10^{-21} \text{ J.}$$

If we take as the base area L^2 of the predicted coloroid implementation the value determined by the speed of light c and the pulse duration τ, this gives the expected length L of elements of a given network of coloroids

$$L = c \times \tau = 3 \times 10^8 \times 5 \times 10^{-15} = 15 \times 10^{-7} \text{ m} = 1500 \text{ nm} = 1.5 \text{ } \mu\text{m.}$$

Let us also approximately take into account the energy E_c directed to a set of the required color of a light filter based on liquid crystals, using the average control power P_c [34] in the value 10^{-8} W/m^2 in for the coloroid area L^2 and obtain $P_c = (10^{-8}) \times (1.5 \times 10^{-6})^2$ $W \approx 2 \times 10^{-20}$ W. Let's assume that the duration of the filter control pulse is $\delta t = 10$ ms, then the required energy will be $E_c = 2 \times 10^{-22}$ J.

It should be taken into account that when constructing nano-sized optical devices, it is also necessary to take into account the wave properties of light. Of course, the estimate proposed by the authors is approximate or, more precisely predictive for assessing the prospects for using the proposed optical computing architecture. At the same time, the assessment of energy costs indicates that they are approaching the lower limit of energy consumption according to Landauer's principle.

It should also be noted that the obtained forecast results are close to the results of assessing the efficiency of network optical computing given in the work [14].

7.6 Conclusion

This work continues research into the development of a computing architecture based on optical devices that work with color information quanta. The fundamental advantages of the proposed approach are shown, which consist of constructing logical operations for evaluating and obtaining solutions directly based on input fuzzy information in the form of color quanta.

Also, one of the advantages of optical computing architecture is a significant reduction in switching devices, which is shown in the proposed implementation options for a coloroid computing network.

The work studies in detail, and makes a comparative analysis of, the number of operations of binary computational procedures and the proposed coloroid computer network for the considered problems of logical inference based on fuzzy input data. It can be concluded that the use of optical computing makes it possible to reduce the number of operations by more than two orders of magnitude.

The theoretical speed of operations with light will be many times higher than using conventional processors, the very representation of optically visible light allows one to bypass the binary bit structure on which modern computing is based. This, in turn, has the potential both for significant miniaturization of devices and for increasing energy efficiency due to the nature of the processes taking place and reducing the number of necessary operations, which is confirmed by calculations.

The most important aspect of the energy efficiency of optical computing, taking into account the possible implementation of its elemental base, is predicted to have a positive value in accordance with Landauer's principle.

Further stages of the developers' research will be aimed at creating logical procedures and decision-making rules and optimizing the computational optical architecture.

Appendix

ARM assembly code (ARMv7-M Thumb instruction set)

```
0800052e:    ldrb.w   r3, [r7, #39]
08000532:    adds     r3, #40
08000534:    add      r3, r7
08000536:    ldrb.w   r2, [r3, #-12]
0800053a:    ldrb.w   r3, [r7, #39]
0800053e:    adds     r3, #40
08000540:    add      r3, r7
08000542:    ldrb.w   r3, [r3, #-24]
08000546:    cmp      r2, r3
08000548:    bcs.n    0x8000564

0800054a:    ldrb.w   r2, [r7, #39]
0800054e:    ldrb.w   r3, [r7, #39]
08000552:    adds     r2, #40
08000554:    add      r2, r7
08000556:    ldrb.w   r2, [r2, #-12]
0800055a:    adds     r3, #40
0800055c:    add      r3, r7
0800055e:    strb.w   r2, [r3, #-36]
08000562:    b.n      0x800057c
08000564:    ldrb.w   r2, [r7, #39]
08000568:    ldrb.w   r3, [r7, #39]
0800056c:    adds     r2, #40
0800056e:    add      r2, r7
08000570:    ldrb.w   r2, [r2, #-24]
08000574:    adds     r3, #40
08000576:    add      r3, r7
08000578:    strb.w   r2, [r3, #-36]
```

x86-x64 assembly code (standard Intel mnemonics)

```
        movzx   eax, BYTE PTR -1[rbp]
        cmp     BYTE PTR -2[rbp], al
        jnb     .L2
        movzx   eax, BYTE PTR -1[rbp]
        mov     BYTE PTR -3[rbp], al
        jmp     .L3
.L2:
        movzx   eax, BYTE PTR -2[rbp]
        mov     BYTE PTR -3[rbp], al
```

References

[1] Y. J. Jung, et al., 'Reconfigurable all-optical logic AND, NAND, OR, NOR, XOR and XNOR gates implemented by photonic crystal nonlinear cavities', 2009 Conference on Lasers & Electro Optics & The Pacific Rim Conference', Shanghai, China, pp. 1-2, 2009, doi:10.1109/CLEOPR.2009.5292059.

[2] S. Ma, Z. Chen, N. K. Dutta, 'All-optical logic gates based on two-photon absorption in semiconductor optical amplifiers', Optics Communications, Vol. 282 (23), pp. 4508-4512, 2009. https://doi.org/10.101 6/j.optcom.2009.08.039

[3] V. Jandieri, R. Khomeriki, et al., 'Functional all-optical logic gates for true time-domain signal processing in nonlinear photonic crystal waveguides', Optics Express, Vol. 28(12), pp. 18317-18331, 2020, https://doi.org/10.1364/OE.395015

[4] X. Wang, et al., 'High-performance spiral all-optical logic gate based on topological edge states of valley photonic crystal', arXiv:2209.08358, 2022. https://doi.org/10.48550/arXiv.2209.08358

[5] L. Caballero, et al., 'Photonic crystalintegrated logic gates and circuits', Optics Express, Vol. 30(2), pp. 1976-1993, 2022, https://doi.org/10.1364/OE.444 714

[6] Z. Zhu, J. Yuan, L. Jiang, 'Multifunctional and multichannels all-optical logic gates based on the in-plane coherent control of localized surface plasmons', Optics letters, Vol. 45(23), pp. 6362-6365, 2020, https://doi:10.136 4/OL.402085

[7] K. Moritaka, T. Kawano, 'Spectroscopic analysis of the model color filters used for computation of CIELAB-based optical logic gates', ICIC Express Letters, Part B: Applications, vol. 5(6), pp. 1715-1720, 2014.

[8]   Z. Lin, M. Hong, 'Femtosecond Laser Precision Engineering: From Micron, Submicron, to Nanoscale', Ultrafast Science, Vol. 2021, Article ID: 9783514, 2021, DOI:10.34133/2021/9783514

[9]   C. Cole, 'Optical and electrical programmable computing energy use comparison', Optics Express, Vol. 29, Issue 9, pp. 13153-13170, 2021.

[10]   J. Hong, et al., 'Bokor, Experimental test of Landauer's principle in single-bit operations on nanomagnetic memory bits', Sci. Adv. 2, e1501492, 2016.

[11]   J. D. Meindl, J. A. Davis, 'The Fundamental Limit on Binary Switching Energy for Terascale Integration (TSI)', IEEE Journal of Solid-State Circuits, Vol. 35, No. 10, pp. 1515- 1516, October 2000, doi:10.1109/4.871332.

[12]   V. Nikul, A. Drozd, J. Drozd, V. Ozeransky, 'Efficiency of the computation bitwise pipelining in FPGA based components of safety-related systems', Technology and design in electronic equipment, no. 4, pp. 3-13, 2018, http://jnas.nbuv.gov.ua/article/UJRN-0000933499

[13]   P. L. McMahon, 'The physics of optical computing', arXiv:2308.00088v1, [physics.optics], 31 July 2023.

[14]   M. Matuszewski, A. Prystupiuk, A. Opala, 'The role of all-optical neural networks', arXiv:2306.06632v2, [cs.ET], 13 June 2023.

[15]   L. Zadeh, 'The role of fuzzy logic in modelling, identification and control', Modelling, Identification and Control, Vol. 15 (3), pp. 191–203, 1994, https://doi:10.4173/mic.1994.3.9

[16]   V. Kreinovich (ed.), 'Uncertainty Modeling', Springer Verlag, Cham, Switzerland, 2017.

[17]   R. Duro, Y. Kondratenko (Eds.), 'Advances in intelligent robotics and collaborative automation', River Publishers, Aalborg, 2015.

[18]   A. I. Shevchenko, 'Natural Human Intelligence - The Object of Research for Artificial Intelligence Creation', International Scientific and Technical Conference on Computer Sciences and Information Technologies, 1, pp. XXVI–XXIX, 8929799, 2019, CSIT 2019, Lviv, 17-20 September 2019.

[19]   Y.P. Kondratenko, O.V. Kozlov, O.V. Korobko, 'Two Modifications of the Automatic Rule Base Synthesis for Fuzzy Control and Decision Making Systems', in: J. Medina et al. (eds), Information Processing and Management of Uncertainty in Knowledge-Based Systems: Theory and Foundations, 17th International Conference, IPMU 2018, Cadiz, Spain, June 11–15, 2018, Proceedings, Part II, CCIS 854, Springer International Publishing AG, pp. 570–582, 2018, https://doi.org/10.1007/978-3-319-91476-3_47

[20]   B. Werners, B., et al., 'Alternative Fuzzy Approaches for Effciently Solving the Capacitated Vehicle Routing Problem in Conditions of Uncertain Demands', in: C. Berger-Vachon, et al. (eds), Complex Systems:

Solutions and Challenges in Economics, Management and Engineering, Studies in Systems, Decision and Control, Vol. 125, Berlin, Heidelberg: Springer International Publishing, pp. 521-543, 2018, https://doi.org/10.1007/978-3-319-69989-9_31

[21] Y. Kondratenko, S. Sidorenko, 'Ship Navigation in Narrowness Passes and Channels in Uncertain Conditions: Intelligent Decision Support', in: P. Shi, J. Stefanovski, J. Kacprzyk (eds), Complex Systems: Spanning Control and Computational Cybernetics: Foundations. Studies in Systems, Decision and Control, vol. 414, Springer, Cham, pp. 475 – 493, 2022, https://doi.org/10.1007/978-3-030-99776-2_24

[22] V. Timchenko, Yu. Kondratenko, V. Kreinovich, 'Why Color Optical Computing?', Studies in Computational Intelligence, 1097, pp. 227–233, 2023, https://doi.org/10.1007/978-3-031-29447-1_20

[23] V. Timchenko, Yu. Kondratenko, V. Kreinovich, 'Interval-Valued and Set-Valued Extensions of Discrete Fuzzy Logics, Belnap Logic, and Color Optical Computing', Lecture Notes in Computer Science (including subseries Lecture Notes in Artificial Intelligence and Lecture Notes in Bioinformatics), 14069 LNCS, pp. 297–303, 2023.

[24] V. Timchenko, Yu. Kondratenko, V. Kreinovich, 'Decision support system for the safety of ship navigation based on optical color logic gates', CEUR Workshop Proceedings, 3347, pp. 42-52, 2022.

[25] V. Timchenko, Yu. Kondratenko, O. Kozlov, V. Kreinovich, 'Fuzzy color computing based on optical logical architecture', Lecture Notes in Networks and Systems, 758 LNNS, pp. 491–498, 2023.

[26] V. Timchenko, Yu. Kondratenko, V. Kreinovich, 'The Architecture of Optical Logical Coloroid with Fuzzy Computing', CEUR Workshop Proceedings, 3373, pp. 638-648, 2023.

[27] V. Timchenko, Yu. Kondratenko, V. Kreinovich, 'Implementation of Optical Logic Gates Based on Color Filters', Lecture Notes on Data Engineering and Communications Technologies, 181, pp. 126–136, 2023.

[28] N. Sulaiman, Z. A. Obaid, M. H. Marhaban, M. N. Hamidon, 'FPGA-Based Fuzzy Logic: Design and Applications – a Review', IACSIT International Journal of Engineering and Technology, Vol. 1, No. 5, pp. 491-503, December 2009.

[29] Y. Kondratenko, E. Gordienko, 'Implementation of the neural networks for adaptive control system on FPGA', Annals of DAAAM for 2012 & Proceeding of the 23th Int. DAAAM Symp. "Intelligent Manufacturing and Automation", Vol. 23, No. 1, B. Katalinic (Ed.), Published by DAAAM International, Vienna, Austria, EU, pp. 0389-0392, 2012.

[30] V. Opanasenko, A. Palahin, S. Zavyalov, 'The FPGA-based problem-oriented on-board processor', Proceedings of the 2019 10th IEEE International Conference on Intelligent Data Acquisition and Advanced

Computing Systems: Technology and Applications, IDAACS 2019, 1, pp. 152–157, 8924360, 2019.

[31] 'Cortex-M4 instructions', ARM Developer, https://developer.arm.com/documentat ion/ddi0439/b/CHDDIGAC.

[32] J. Yiu, 'System-on-Chip Design with Arm Cortex-M Processor', eBook, ISBN 978-1-911531-19-7, https://www.arm.com/resources/ebook/system-on-chip-design

[33] A. Fog, 'Instruction tables: Lists of instruction latencies, throughputs and micro-operation breakdowns for Intel, AMD and VIA CPUs', 2023, https: //www.agner.org/optimize/instruction_tables.pdf.

[34] M. Gritsenko, 'Physics of Liquid Crystals, Taras Shevchenko ChNPU', Chernigiv, 2015, erpub.chnpu.edu.ua:8080/jspui/handle/123456789/7138

Authors' Short CV

Victor Timchenko received his master's degree in Electrical Engineering from Admiral Makarov National University of Shipbuilding (AMNUS) in 1982, hi philosophy of doctorate degree in Design of Ships from AMNUS in 1988, and doctor of science degree in Automation Control from Odessa National Polytechnic University in 2013. He is currently working as a Professor at the Department of Computer Engineering at Automation and Electrical Institute of AMNUS. His research areas include robust optimal control systems, optical architecture and computing, and decision support systems.

Vladik Kreinovich, Professor of Computer Science, University of Texas at El Paso, El Paso, Texas, USA, Vice President of International Fuzzy Systems Association (IFSA) and Vice President of European Society of Fuzzy Logic and Technology (EUSFLAT), AT&T Fellow in Information Technology. Areas of interest: interval computations, intelligent control (including fuzzy and neural approaches), reasoning under uncertainty. He is the author of more than 1500 publications.

Yuriy Kondratenko is a Doctor of Science, Professor, Honour Inventor of Ukraine (2008), Corr. Academician of Royal Academy of Doctors (Barcelona, Spain), Head of the Department of Intelligent Information Systems at Petro Mohyla Black Sea National University (PMBSNU), Ukraine, Leading Researcher of the Institute of Artificial Intelligence Problems of MES and NAS of Ukraine, Fulbright Scholar. He received a Ph.D. (1983) and Dr.Sc. (1994) at Odessa National Polytechnic University, and several international grants and scholarships for conducting research at P.R. of China, Germany, and the USA. Research interests include robotics, automation, sensors and control systems, intelligent decision support systems, and fuzzy logic.

Volodymyr Horbov graduated in January 2021 from the Department of Computer Control Systems at the Admiral Makarov National University of Shipbuilding, Ukraine with a master's degree in Automation and Computer-Integrated Technologies. Now, he is a control theory postgraduate student at the Department of Marine Instrumentation of the Admiral Makarov National University of Shipbuilding, Ukraine. Mr. Horbov is a specialist in control systems, programming and radio electronic engineering. His research interests include control systems, marine and air autonomous drones.

Index

Printed in the United States
by Baker & Taylor Publisher Services